THE DELICIOUS
GREEN MOUNTAIN
WOOD PELLET GRILL
COOKBOOK

1000-DAY RECIPES FOR YOUR WOOD PELLET GRILL TO ENJOY EVERYTHING FROM ... BBQ DISHES

JUDY REILLY

Copyright © 2021 by Judy Reilly- All rights reserved.

The content contained within this book may not be reproduced, duplicated, or transmitted without direct written permission from the author or the publisher. Under no circumstances will any blame or legal responsibility be held against the publisher, or author, for any damages, reparation, or monetary loss due to the information contained within this book, either directly or indirectly.

<u>Legal Notice</u>: This book is copyright protected. It is only for personal use. You cannot amend, distribute, sell, use, quote or paraphrase any part, or the content within this book, without the consent of the author or publisher.

<u>Disclaimer Notice</u>: Please note the information contained within this document is for educational and entertainment purposes only. All effort has been executed to present accurate, up to date, reliable, complete information. No warranties of any kind are declared or implied. Readers acknowledge that the author is not engaged in the rendering of legal, financial, medical, or professional advice. The content within this book has been derived from various sources. Please consult a licensed professional before attempting any techniques outlined in this book. By reading this document, the reader agrees that under no circumstances is the author responsible for any losses, direct or indirect, that are incurred as a result of the use of the information contained within this document, including, but not limited to, errors, omissions, or inaccuracies.

CONTENTS

INTRODUCTION

What Wood Pellet Grills Are

A wood pellet grill is basically a hybrid between a smoker, a traditional grill, and an oven. They can be used for many different types of cooking, even searing and baking. Wood pellets are used for fuel. Some wood pellets are meant to last a long time, while others focus on enhancing flavor.
Pellet grills do not cook food over a direct flame. Instead, they heat food indirectly by circulating the warmth through the grill, much like what an oven does.

How the Green Mountain Wood Pellet Grill Works

A pellet grill looks like a gas grill, with a metal hopper mounted to one side to house the wood pellets they burn as fuel. The resulting fire imparts a smoky taste because the wood pellets are made from flavorful hardwood species such as hickory, oak, pecan, and cherry.
Today's pellet grills feature an electronic thermostat with a digital display, so you can dial in a precise cooking temperature; the hopper automatically draws the appropriate amount of pellets into the firebox, where they're ignited. The grill holds the temperature steady, like an oven, adjusting the rate at which it burns pellets to maintain that set temperature.

The Benefits You'll Gain from Your Green Mountain Wood Pellet Grill

There are some key advantages to be enjoyed when using a pellet smoker. We've covered the most important below.

1. A pellet smoker offers more options and versatility than a standard smoker. Depending on the model you choose, it will be possible to roast, smoke, barbecue, and even bake inside your pellet smoker.

2. Pellet smoking offers the best results for smoked meat. This is because they are designed specifically to infuse maximum smoke flavor with indirect heat. When compared to smoking in a normal grill, the results are far better. For rich and complex flavor, a dedicated pellet smoker is an ideal choice.

3. Flavor options are virtually unlimited. Pellet chips are made from natural wood pieces, with flavors like hickory, maple, apple, mesquite, cherry, and more.

4. Temperature management is simple because most pellet smokers have advanced designs with automatic timing and heat control. The hopper ensures a consistent level of smoke throughout cooking.
5. Most models reach smoking temperature within ten to fifteen minutes. Only gas grills are easier and faster to get to cooking temperature.
6. Pellet smokers are designed for serious home cooks, so they are generally large, offering plenty of cooking space. This means you can easily cook whole turkeys, chicken, duck and other game, large BBQ cuts, and anything else that you want to infuse with a rich flavor.
7. Unlike a charcoal or gas smoker, pellet models are easy to use. There's no need to measure or weigh the wood that you will use. Pellets are distributed as needed and cooking temperature is regulated by an electronic thermostat.
8. Value is incredible because a high-quality pellet smoker will last for many years without problems. Even though the initial price might be higher than a comparable gas or charcoal grill, longevity, ease of use, and amazing results add value.

Using Tips for Your Green Mountain Wood Pellet Grill

1. Take advantage of your pellet grill's searing capabilities.

Many pellet grills feature searing capabilities, meaning they can reach temperatures over 500 degrees. Again, check your owner's manual for information on your specific model.

2. Use lower temperatures to generate more smoke.

You'll generate more smoke at lower temperatures, particularly in the "low and slow" range between 225 and 275.

3. Use the reverse sear method.

Don't be afraid to smoke your meat at a lower temperature, then finish it at a higher temperature. This two-step approach is especially useful for smoking chicken with crisp (not rubbery) skin, or the "reverse sear method" often employed for thicker steaks or prime rib

4. Never allow the pellets in the pellet hopper to run out.

Never allow the pellets in the pellet hopper to run out. If this happens, consult your owner's manual before relighting the grill. If you must, set a timer to remind yourself to top off the pellets.

5. Experiment with pellet flavors.

Experiment with pellet flavors. Some brands of pellets are fairly subtle.

Better to Clean Your Green Mountain Wood Pellet Grill

It is often easiest to clean the inside of your grill at the same time as the outside because your grill will already be unplugged, cold and emptied of wood pellets. Cleaning the inside of your pellet smoker involves several steps to ensure proper pellet grill maintenance, including cleaning the grease drip tray, vacuuming and scraping the burn pot and scrubbing the grill grates.

1. GREASE DRIP TRAY

To clean the grease drip tray, first remove the grill grates and any extra cooking racks. Use a griddle scraper to scrub grease off of the surface of the tray and remove the scrubbed grease using a paper towel. Wipe the grease drip tray clean using a cloth or paper towel. If you want to clean your grease drip tray with soapy water or liquid cleaner, remove the tray from the BBQ first. Dry the tray completely before putting it back into your pellet smoker.

2. BURN POT

Regular pellet grill ash clean-out keeps your smoker operating in top condition. A clean smoker provides even cooking and produce the best tasting pulled pork, ribs, and grilled veggies — or anything else you want to cook.

To clean your burn pot, first remove the grease drip tray and heat deflector to access the burn pot. Pay attention to how they are installed so you can put them back in when you are done. The burn pot will often have a lot of ash build-up and debris that you will need to remove. The simplest way to clean your pellet smoker's burn pot is with a vacuum cleaner or ash vac. Use the hose to suck out all the ash and then wipe away any remaining ash or soot using a clean rag.

When deep cleaning your pellet grill after winter, you can take this a few steps further and scrub the interior walls of the smoker to remove any accumulated grease or dirt. After vacuuming the ash, use a scraper with a flat edge to dislodge scale from the sides of the smoker chamber. Scrub the loosened dirt with a non-metallic brush and wipe the fire pot with a clean cloth.

You can use a damp cloth to wipe the interior of the grill, but never put water directly into the burn pot. Use caution not to damage the electric elements and allow the grill to dry completely before use. Once your burn pot is clean, replace the heat deflector, drip tray, and grates.

If your grill is equipped with an ash container, now is a great time to empty it. Ash collection systems make it easy to remove ash build-up and allow you to clean your burn pot less often, as they collect much of the ash that normally builds up inside your pellet smoker.

3. GRILL GRATES

Cleaning your pellet smoker grates every time you use your grill keeps your food tasting delicious and fresh so your cookout guests are always satisfied. There are two ways to clean your grill grates; cold or hot. Follow these steps for how to clean your grill before or after use:

Cold Method (Before Cooking):

Ensure your grill is unplugged and cool:

Remove grates from grill and clean with bbq degreaser or soap and water. Some pellet grills may have dishwasher safe grates. If not, they can be cleaned in a sink or with a pressure washer or garden hose. If they are painted, be careful with using a pressure washer.

Scrub the grates thoroughly: Use a brush or spatula to scrub the grates to remove any residue that remains.

Hot Method (After Cooking):

Set your grill to the highest temperature: Grill grates are easiest to clean when they are hot — and your grill will do most of the work for you. After you cook, turn your grill to the highest temperature and allow it to heat up completely.

Do a burn off: Wait 10 to 15 minutes to let your grill burn away the remaining food and grease on the grill grates. Performing a burn off loosens any stuck-on grease and makes it easy to scrape off the ash.

Scrub the grates thoroughly: Use a brush or spatula to scrub the grates to remove any residue that remains. Because the grill will be hot, it is best to use a long-handled brush or scraper. You may also choose to clean your grill grates while wearing an oven mitt or grill glove to prevent burns.

SEAFOOD RECIPES

Honey Balsamic Salmon

Servings: 2

Cooking Time: 25 Minutes

Ingredients:

- ➢ 1 Medium salmon fillet
- ➢ Fin & Feather Rub
- ➢ 1/2 Cup balsamic vinegar
- ➢ 1 Tablespoon minced garlic
- ➢ 2 Tablespoon honey

Directions:

1. Season the fillet with the Traeger Fin & Feather Rub.

2. Make the glaze: Combine the vinegar, garlic and honey in a small saucepan. Simmer over medium heat until reduced by half. Usually 10 to 15 minutes. The glaze will be properly reduced when it coats the back of a spoon. Using a basting brush, coat the fillet with the glaze.

3. Supply your smoker with wood pellets and follow the start-up procedure. Preheat the grill, with the lid closed, to 350° F.

4. Arrange the salmon fillet on the grill grate. Grill for 25 to 30 minutes, or until the salmon is opaque and flakes easily with a fork. Grill: 350 °F

5. Transfer to a platter or plates and serve immediately. If desired, heat any remaining glaze to a boil and drizzle over top of the salmon. Enjoy!

Smoke-roasted Halibut With Mixed Herb Vinaigrette

Servings: 4

Cooking Time: 12 Minutes

Ingredients:

- ➤ 4 halibut fillets, each about 6 to 8oz (170 to 225g)
- ➤ for the vinaigrette
- ➤ 2 tbsp white wine vinegar or sherry vinegar, plus more
- ➤ ¼ tsp coarse salt, plus more
- ➤ ¼ tsp freshly ground black pepper, plus more
- ➤ ½ cup extra virgin olive oil
- ➤ 2 tbsp minced fresh herbs, such as dill, flat-leaf parsley, or oregano
- ➤ for serving
- ➤ 4 cups loosely packed baby arugula, spinach, or other mixed greens
- ➤ 1 lemon, cut lengthwise into 4 wedges

Directions:

1. Supply your smoker with wood pellets and follow the start-up procedure. Preheat the grill, with the lid closed, to 400° F.

2. In a small bowl, make the vinaigrette by whisking together the vinegar, and salt and pepper. Whisk until the salt dissolves. Continue to whisk while slowly adding the olive oil. Whisk until the vinaigrette is emulsified. Stir in the herbs. Taste, adding vinegar or salt and pepper to taste. Pour 1/3 of the vinaigrette into a separate container. Reserve the remainder.

3. Place the fillets on a rimmed sheet pan. Lightly brush both sides with the smaller portion of vinaigrette. (Dividing the vinaigrette into two containers prevents cross-contamination.) Lightly season with salt and pepper.

4. Place the fillets on the grate at an angle to the bars. Grill until the edges begin to look opaque, about 4 to 6 minutes. Gently turn and grill until the fish is cooked through, about 4 to 6 minutes more. (A fillet will break into clean flakes when pressed with a fork when it's done.)

5. Remove the fish from the grill. Place the greens in a large bowl and toss them with 2 to 3 tablespoons of the reserved vinaigrette (you want the greens lightly coated) and divide between 4 plates. Place a fillet on the greens on each plate. Drizzle a bit more of the vinaigrette over the top. Serve with lemon wedges.

Lobster Tail

Servings: 2

Cooking Time: 25 Minutes

Ingredients:

- 2 lobster tails
- Salt
- Freshly ground black pepper
- 1 batch Lemon Butter Mop for Seafood

Directions:

1. Supply your smoker with wood pellets and follow the start-up procedure. Preheat the grill, with the lid closed, to 375°F.

2. Using kitchen shears, slit the top of the lobster shells, through the center, nearly to the tail. Once cut, expose as much meat as you can through the cut shell.

3. Season the lobster tails all over with salt and pepper.

4. Place the tails directly on the grill grate and grill until their internal temperature reaches 145°F. Remove the lobster from the grill and serve with the mop on the side for dipping.

Barbecued Scallops

Servings: 4

Cooking Time: 10 Minutes

Ingredients:

➢   1 pound large scallops

➢   2 tablespoons olive oil

➢   1 batch Dill Seafood Rub

Directions:

1.   Supply your smoker with wood pellets and follow the start-up procedure. Preheat the grill, with the lid closed, to 375°F.

2.   Coat the scallops all over with olive oil and season all sides with the rub.

3.   Place the scallops directly on the grill grate and grill for 5 minutes per side. Remove the scallops from the grill and serve immediately.

Grilled Mussels With Lemon Butter

Servings: 4

Cooking Time: 15 Minutes

Ingredients:

- 2 Pound Mussels, debearded, washed
- 5 Quart water
- 1/3 Cup salt
- 2 Clove garlic, minced
- 1/3 Cup white wine
- 1 Whole lemon juice
- 3 Tablespoon parsley, chopped
- 1 loaf French country bread

Directions:

1. Supply your smoker with wood pellets and follow the start-up procedure. Preheat the grill, with the lid closed, to 375° F.

2. Scrub mussels well in running water making sure to remove all dirt and barnacles.

3. Place clean mussels in a large bowl with 5 quarts (5 L) water and 1/3 cup (91 g) of salt for about 15 minutes.

4. Drain, rinse and repeat soaking method two more times to purge and remove all sand.

5. Melt butter in a saute pan over medium high heat. Add garlic and cook for 1 minute until fragrant. Add wine and bring to a simmer. Add mussels and lemon juice to the pan and toss to coat.

6. Cover with a tight fitting lid and transfer to the grill. Let the mussels steam 8-10 minutes. Remove from the grill and discard any unopened mussels.

7. Sprinkle with chopped parsley and transfer to a serving dish. Serve with sliced bread. Enjoy!

Grilled Lemon Salmon

Servings: 4

Cooking Time: 60 Minutes

Ingredients:

➢ Dill, Fresh

➢ 1 Lemon, Sliced

➢ 1 1/2 - 2 Lbs Salmon, Fresh

Directions:

1. Supply your smoker with wood pellets and follow the start-up procedure. Preheat the grill, with the lid closed, to 225° F.

2. Place the salmon on a cedar plank. Lay the lemon slices along the top of the salmon. Smoke in your Grill for about 60 minutes.

3. Top with fresh dill and serve.

Simple Glazed Salmon Fillets

Servings: 2

Cooking Time: 25 Minutes

Ingredients:

- 4 (6-8 oz) center-cut salmon fillets, skin on
- Fin & Feather Rub
- 1/2 Cup mayonnaise
- 2 Tablespoon Dijon mustard
- 1 Tablespoon fresh lemon juice
- 1 Tablespoon fresh chopped tarragon or dill
- lemon wedges

Directions:

1. Season the fillets with the Traeger Fin & Feather Rub.

2. Make the Glaze: Combine the mayonnaise and mustard in a small bowl. Stir in the lemon juice and dill or tarragon.

3. Spread the flesh-side of the fillets with the glaze.

4. Supply your smoker with wood pellets and follow the start-up procedure. Preheat the grill, with the lid closed, to 350° F.

5. Arrange the salmon fillets on the grill grate, skin-side down. Grill for 25 to 30 minutes, or until the salmon is opaque and flakes easily with a fork. Grill: 350 °F

6. Transfer to a platter or plates, garnish with sliced lemons and chopped dill and serve immediately. Enjoy!

Grilled Trout With Citrus & Basil

Servings: 4

Cooking Time: 10 Minutes

Ingredients:

- 6 Whole Trout
- 2 Teaspoon Blackened Saskatchewan Rub
- 10 Sprig fresh basil
- 2 Lemons, cut in half
- extra-virgin olive oil

Directions:

1. Supply your smoker with wood pellets and follow the start-up procedure. Preheat the grill, with the lid closed, to 450° F.

2. Season the center cavity of the trout with the Traeger Blackened Saskatchewan. Place two sprigs of Basil in each cavity, then add 4 lemon halves.

3. Next tie the fish closed using the Butchers twine, and then rub with olive oil.

4. Place the trout on the hot grill and cook 5 minutes on each side. Enjoy! Grill: 450 ˚F

Mezcal Shrimp With Salsa De Molcajete

Servings: 4

Cooking Time: 14 Minutes

Ingredients:

- 18 to 24 jumbo shrimp, about 1½lb (680g) total, peeled and deveined
- ⅓ cup mezcal
- juice of ½ lime
- 2 tbsp extra virgin olive oil
- 2 tsp coarse salt
- 1 tsp ground cumin
- lime wedges
- for the salsa
- 2 Roma tomatoes
- 2 tomatillos, husked and washed
- 2 garlic cloves, peeled and impaled on a toothpick
- 1 jalapeño or serrano pepper
- 1 small white onion, halved
- ½ tsp coarse salt, plus more
- juice of ½ lime
- ¼ cup loosely packed fresh cilantro leaves

Directions:

1. Supply your smoker with wood pellets and follow the start-up procedure. Preheat the grill, with the lid closed, to 450° F.

2. In a large bowl, combine the shrimp, mezcal, lime juice, olive oil, salt, and ground cumin. Toss with your hands to mix thoroughly. Set aside for 15 minutes and then toss once more.

3. Begin to make the salsa by placing the tomatoes, tomatillos, garlic, jalapeño, and onion on the grate. Grill until they begin to char, about 3 minutes for the garlic and about 6 to 8 minutes for the other vegetables, turning as needed. Transfer the vegetables to a rimmed sheet pan. Remove the skewers from the garlic. Let everything cool. Coarsely chop the vegetables and leave them in separate piles.

4. Place the garlic in the molcajete and add the salt. Mash the garlic to a purée using the temolote. Add the onion and grind it into the garlic paste. Stir in the jalapeño (deseeded for a milder salsa), tomatoes, and tomatillos. Stir in the lime juice and cilantro leaves. Taste, adding salt. (If you don't own a molcajete or temolote, prepare the salsa using a small food processor.)

5. Drain the shrimp and discard the marinade. Thread the shrimp on wood or bamboo skewers. Place the shrimp on the grate and grill until they're white and opaque, about 4 to 6 minutes, tossing with tongs.

6. Transfer the shrimp to a platter. Serve with the salsa and lime wedges.

Roasted Halibut With Spring Vegetables

Servings: 4

Cooking Time: 20 Minutes

Ingredients:

- 4 thick-cut halibut fillets
- 2 Tablespoon Fin & Feather Rub
- Butcher Paper
- 1 Pound Carrots, Peeled and Cut into 3/4" Inch Slices
- 1 Pound asparagus, ends trimmed
- 1/2 Pound Oyster Mushrooms
- 2 Tablespoon butter
- salt and pepper
- 1/2 Cup white wine

Directions:

1. Season the halibut fillets with Traeger Fin and Feather Rub.

2. To build the packets: Start with four sheets of parchment paper about twenty inches long. Fold in half, then open it back up.

3. Divide the carrots, asparagus, and mushrooms between the four pieces of parchment and top each with a little bit of butter. Season with salt and pepper. Place a halibut fillet on top of the vegetables in each packet.

4. Next, fold the paper over so the two ends meet, enclosing the food. Beginning at either end of the center crease, make small, overlapping diagonal folds around the filling, sealing the packet tight. Before finishing the final fold, pour a little bit of wine in each packet then seal completely.

5. Supply your smoker with wood pellets and follow the start-up procedure. Preheat the grill, with the lid closed, to 500° F.

6. Place all four packets on a sheet tray and place in the grill. Cook for 7-10 minutes or until the internal temperature of the fish reaches 145°F. Remove from the grill and place packet on a serving dish. Grill: 500 °F Probe: 145 °F

7. Using a knife or scissors, cut open each packet and fold the edges back. Finish with a little bit of lemon juice if desired. Enjoy!

Grilled Lobster Tails With Smoked Paprika Butter

Servings: 4

Cooking Time: 10-12 Minutes

Ingredients:

- 4 lobster tails, each about 8 to 10oz (225 to 285g), thawed if frozen
- 3 lemons, 1 quartered lengthwise, 2 halved through their equators
- for the butter
- 1¼ cup unsalted butter, at room temperature
- 2 garlic cloves, peeled and finely minced
- 3 tbsp chopped fresh parsley
- 2 tbsp chopped fresh chives
- 1 tbsp freshly squeezed lemon juice
- 2 tsp finely chopped lemon zest
- 2 tsp smoked paprika
- 1 tsp coarse salt

Directions:

1. Supply your smoker with wood pellets and follow the start-up procedure. Preheat the grill, with the lid closed, to 450° F.

2. In a medium bowl, make the paprika butter by combining the ingredients. Beat with a wooden spoon until well blended.

3. Use a sharp, heavy knife or sturdy kitchen shears to cut lengthwise through the top shell of each lobster tail in a straight line toward the tail fin. Gently loosen the meat from the bottom shell and sides. Lift the meat through the slit you just made so the meat sits on top of the shell. Slip a lemon quarter underneath the meat (between the meat and the bottom shell) to keep it elevated. Spread 1 tablespoon of paprika butter on top of each lobster. Melt the remaining butter and keep it warm.

4. Place the lobster tails flesh side up and lemon halves cut sides down on the grate. Grill the lobsters until the flesh is white and opaque and the internal temperature of the lobster meat reaches 135 to 140°F (57 to 60°C), about 10 to 12 minutes, basting at least once with some of the melted butter. (Don't overcook or the lobster will become unpleasantly rubbery.)

5. Transfer the lobsters and the lemon halves to a platter. Divide the remaining melted butter between 4 ramekins before serving.

Bacon Wrapped Scallops

Servings: 8

Cooking Time: 20 Minutes

Ingredients:

- ➢ 24 jumbo deep sea diver scallops, dry-packed
- ➢ 1/2 Cup butter
- ➢ salt
- ➢ freshly ground black pepper
- ➢ 1 Clove garlic, minced
- ➢ 12 Slices thin-cut bacon, cut in half crosswise
- ➢ lemon wedges, for serving

Directions:

1. Remove the small, crescent-shaped muscle from the side of each scallop, if still attached. Dry the scallops thoroughly on paper towels, then transfer to a medium bowl.

2. Melt butter in a small saucepan, add garlic and cook for 1 minute. Let cool slightly then pour over the scallops. Season with salt and pepper and gently toss to coat.

3. Wrap a piece of bacon around each scallop and secure with a toothpick.

4. Supply your smoker with wood pellets and follow the start-up procedure. Preheat the grill, with the lid closed, to 400° F.

5. Arrange the scallops directly on the grill grate. Grill for 15 to 20 minutes, or until the scallop is opaque and the bacon has begun to crisp. If desired, you can turn the scallops on their side, bacon-side down, turning occasionally to crisp the bacon. Do not overcook. Grill: 400 °F

6. Transfer the scallops to a platter and serve with lemon wedges.

Seared Ahi Tuna Steak With Soy Sauce

Servings: 2

Cooking Time: 60 Minutes

Ingredients:

- 1/2 Cup Gluten Free Soy Sauce
- 1 Large Sushi Grade Ahi Tuna Steak, Patted Dry
- 1/4 Cup Lime Juice
- 2 Tablespoons Rice Wine Vinegar
- 2 Tablespoons Sesame Oil, Divided
- 2 Tablespoons Sriracha Sauce
- 4 Tablespoons Sweet Heat Rub
- 2 Cups Water

Directions:

1. Supply your smoker with wood pellets and follow the start-up procedure. Preheat the grill, with the lid closed, to 400° F. If using gas or charcoal, set it up for high heat over direct heat.

2. In the glass baking dish, pour in the water, soy sauce, lime juice, rice wine vinegar, 1 tablespoon sesame oil, sriracha sauce, and mirin. Whisk the marinade together with the whisk until everything is well combine. Place the ahi steak into the marinade and place the glass baking dish with the ahi steak in the refrigerator for 30 minutes. After 30 minutes, flip the ahi steak over so that the ahi has the chance to fully marinate on all sides, and allow to marinate for 30 more minutes.

3. After the tuna steak has finished marinating, drain off the marinade and pat the steak dry with paper towels on all sides. Pour the Sweet Heat Rub onto the plate and rub the remaining tablespoon of sesame oil generously on all sides of the tuna steak, and then gently place the tuna steak into the seasoning on the plate, turning on all sides to coat evenly.

4. Insert a temperature probe into the thickest part of the ahi steak and place the steak on the hottest part of the grill. Grill the ahi tuna steak for 45 seconds on each side, or just until the outside is opaque and has grill marks. Flip the steak and allow it to grill for another 45 seconds until the outside is just cooked through. The ahi tuna steak's internal temperature should be just at 115°F.

5. Remove the steak from the grill once it reaches 115°F, and immediately slice and serve. The inside of the steak should still be cool and ruby pink.

Oysters In The Shell

Servings: 4

Cooking Time: 20 Minutes

Ingredients:

- ➢ 8 medium oysters, unopened, in the shell, rinsed and scrubbed
- ➢ 1 batch Lemon Butter Mop for Seafood

Directions:

1. Supply your smoker with wood pellets and follow the start-up procedure. Preheat the grill, with the lid closed, to 375°F.

2. Place the unopened oysters directly on the grill grate and grill for about 20 minutes, or until the oysters are done and their shells open.

3. Discard any oysters that do not open. Shuck the remaining oysters, transfer them to a bowl, and add the mop. Serve immediately.

BAKING RECIPES

Pineapple Cake

Servings: 4

Cooking Time: 30 Minutes

Ingredients:

- 2/3 cup of vegetable oil (olive oil works great, not virgin)
- 3 eggs
- 1/3 cup brown sugar (not too sweet)
- 3/4 cup self raising plain flour
- 1/4 cup wholemeal self raising flour
- 1/3 cup saltanas
- 1/3 cup diced canned pineapple (drained)
- 1/3 cup diced raw walnuts
- 2 large carrots grated
- Icing Ingredients
- 250 grams cream cheese
- 35 grams icing sugar (not too sweet)
- Whole lemon or orange zest

Directions:

1. Mix all ingredients in a large bowl.
2. Place into 6″ greased baking tray or un-greased silicone tray.
3. Supply your smoker with wood pellets and follow the start-up procedure. Preheat the grill, with the lid closed, to 190 °F. Cook for 25-30min until golden brown and no dough when probed.
4. Let cool on rack (not directly on plate or board) then apply icing.
5. Whip icing ingredients and place in fridge until ready to coat the cake.

Blueberry Pancakes

Servings: 4

Cooking Time: 10 Minutes

Ingredients:

- 2 Cups Blueberries, Fresh
- 1 Cup Pancake Mix
- 1/2 Cup Sugar
- 3/4 Cup Water, Warm

Directions:

1. Supply your smoker with wood pellets and follow the start-up procedure. Preheat the grill, with the lid closed, to 350° F.

2. Place the cast iron griddle on the grates of your grill.

3. In a large bowl, pour water, pancake mix and 1/2 cup of the blueberries and mix until combined.

4. Pour the batter onto the griddle in 4 equal parts. Cook with the lid closed for about 6 minutes, or until the edges of the pancakes are slightly cooked. Flip each pancake and continue cooking for another 4 minutes.

5. Pour the hot blueberry sauce over your freshly cooked pancakes and enjoy!

Spiced Carrot Cake

Servings: 10   Cooking Time: 35 Minutes

Ingredients:

- 1/2 Cup Apple Sauce, Unsweetened
- 2 Tsp Baking Powder
- 1 Tsp Baking Soda
- 1 1/2 Cups Brown Sugar
- 1/2 Cup Butter, Room Temp
- 3/4 Cup Canola Oil
- 3 Cups Carrot, Grated
- 1 1/2 Tsp Cinnamon, Ground
- 2 (8-Ounce) Packages Cream Cheese, Room Temperature
- 4 Egg
- 2 Cups Flour, All-Purpose
- 1/2 Tsp Ginger, Ground
- 1/4 Tsp Nutmeg, Ground
- 1/2 Tsp Salt
- 1/2 Cup Sugar
- 3 Cups Sugar, Icing

Directions:

1. Supply your smoker with wood pellets and follow the start-up procedure. Preheat the grill, with the lid closed, to 350° F.

2. Line the bottom of 2 9-inch cake pans with parchment paper and spray the sides with cooking spray. Set aside.

3. In a large bowl, combine flour, baking powder and soda, spices and salt.

4. In a smaller bowl, combine oil, eggs, sugars, and applesauce and whisk together. Add carrots and stir until well combined.

5. Pour the wet ingredients into the dry. Stir until combined but take care not to over mix. Pour the batter evenly between the two cake pans. Bake for about 35 minutes in your Grill, rotating the cake pans halfway between the cook. Remove once a toothpick is inserted in the middle of the cake and comes out clean.

6. While the cake is cooling, prepare the frosting. Beat the cream cheese until smooth with a hand mixer. Add the butter and icing sugar and mix until fully combined.

7. On a clean plate or cake stand, place one half of the cake and top with a good layer of cream cheese frosting. Place the second half on top and cover with the remaining frosting. Icing tip: try not to lift your knife while icing. Instead make long, smooth strokes. Lifting the knife often make cause crumbs to get into your icing. Top with pecans if desired.

Spiced Lemon Cherry Pie

Servings: 6-8

Cooking Time: 60 Minutes

Ingredients:

- 1/2 Teaspoon Cinnamon, Ground
- 1/2 Teaspoon Cloves, Ground
- 1/2 Cup Cornstarch
- 1 Pound Frozen Sweet Dark Cherries, Thawed
- 1 Teaspoon Water (Beaten With Egg) 1 Egg
- 1 Lemon, Juice
- 1 Lemon, Zest
- 2 Prepared Store Bought Or Homemade Pie Crust
- 1 Teaspoon Hickory Honey Sea Salt Seasoning
- 1 Cup Sugar, Granulated
- 1 Teaspoon Vanilla Extract

Directions:

1. In a large bowl, mix together the thawed cherries and their juices, sugar, cornstarch, lemon zest, lemon juice, cinnamon, clove, vanilla extract and Hickory Honey Sea Salt. Allow to sit for 30 minutes.

2. Flour a work surface and roll out one of the prepared pie crusts so that it fits a 9 inch pie tin. Fill with the cherry pie filling and refrigerate. When the pie is chilled, roll out the second pie crust, brush the edge of the first pie crust with the egg mixture, top with the second pie crust, crimp the edge with a fork, and chill. Alternatively, cut the second pie crust into strips and form a lattice pattern, attaching the strips with the egg mixture. Chill the pie for 15-30 minutes, or until the dough is very cold and firm. Brush the top of the pie with the remaining egg mixture.

3. Supply your smoker with wood pellets and follow the start-up procedure. Preheat the grill, with the lid closed, to 350° F and grill for 45 minutes to 1 hour, or until the pie crust is golden and firm and the filling is bubbly. Remove from the grill and allow to cool at room temperature for at least 4 hours to set the filling, then serve and enjoy!

Eggs Ham Benedict

Servings: 6

Cooking Time: 15 Minutes

Ingredients:

- ➤ 1 Biscuit Dough, Tube
- ➤ 6 Egg
- ➤ 16 Ham, Sliced
- ➤ 1 Packet Hollandaise Sauce, Package

Directions:

1. Supply your smoker with wood pellets and follow the start-up procedure. Preheat the grill, with the lid closed, to 350° F.

2. Grease a muffin tin and crack an egg in each cup. Place on the grate of the for about 10 minutes or until the whites are fully cooked.

3. At the same time, place your biscuit dough on a greased pan. Follow the directions on the packaging but bake on the . Place 2 slices of ham per biscuit on the pan as well.

4. While the ham, eggs, and biscuits are cooking, prepare the Hollandaise Sauce according to the directions on the packet.

5. When everything is fully cooked, cut a biscuit in half, and stack one or two slices of ham, 1 egg and a dollop of Hollandaise sauce. Repeat for each half biscuit. Serve with fresh fruit.

Smoker Wheat Bread

Servings: 6   Cooking Time: 60 Minutes

Ingredients:

- As Needed extra-virgin olive oil
- 2 Cup all-purpose flour
- 1 Cup whole wheat flour
- 1 1/4 Ounce Packet, Active Dry Yeast
- 1 1/4 Teaspoon salt
- 1 1/2 Cup water
- As Needed Cornmeal

Directions:

1. Oil a large mixing bowl and set aside. In a second mixing bowl, combine the flours, yeast, and salt.
2. Push your sleeve up to your elbow and form your fingers into a claw. Mix the dry ingredients until well-combined.
3. Add the water and mix until blended. The dough will be wet, shaggy, and somewhat stringy.
4. Tip the dough into the oiled mixing bowl and cover with plastic wrap.
5. Allow the dough to rise at room temperature-- about 70 degrees-- for 2 hours, or until the surface is bubbled.
6. Turn the dough out onto a lightly floured work surface and lightly flour the top. With floured hands, fold the dough over on itself twice. Cover loosely with plastic wrap and allow the dough to rest for 15 minutes.
7. Dust a clean lint-free cotton towel with cornmeal, wheat bran, or flour. With floured hands, gently form the dough into a ball and place it, seam side down, on the towel.
8. Dust the top of the ball with cornmeal, wheat bran, or flour, and cover the dough with a second towel. Let the dough rise until doubled in size; the dough will not spring back when poked with a finger.
9. In the meantime, start the smoker grill and set temperature to 450 F. Preheat, lid closed, for 10-15 minutes.
10. Put a lidded 6- to 8-quart cast iron Dutch oven - preferably one coated with enamel, on the grill grate.
11. When the dough has risen, remove the top towel, slide your hand under the bottom towel to support the dough, then carefully tip the dough, seam side up, into the preheated pot.
12. Remove the towel. Shake the pot a couple of times if the dough looks lopsided: It will straighten out as it bakes.
13. Cover the pot with the lid and bake the bread for 30 minutes. Remove the lid and continue to bake the bread for 15 to 30 minutes more, or until it is nicely browned and sounds hollow when rapped with your knuckles.
14. Turn onto a wire rack to cool. Slice with a serrated knife. Enjoy!

Cherry Ice Cream Cobbler

Servings: 8

Cooking Time: 45 Minutes

Ingredients:

- 1 Tsp Baking Powder
- 3 Tbsp Butter, Melted
- 1 Cup Flour
- Ice Cream, Prepared
- 1/4 Tsp Salt
- 3/4 Cup Sugar
- 1/2 Cup Milk

Directions:

1. Supply your smoker with wood pellets and follow the start-up procedure. Preheat the grill, with the lid closed, to 350° F.

2. In a bowl, combine flour, sugar, baking powder, salt and mix to incorporate. Stir in butter and milk and mix until combined. In a cast iron pan, dump in cherry pie filling and pile on the prepared topping to cover.

3. Place in your Grill and bake for about 45 minutes, or until the topping is golden brown.

4. Let cool for a couple minutes and serve with ice cream.

Vanilla Cheesecake Skillet Brownie

Servings: 2

Cooking Time: 30 Minutes

Ingredients:

- 1 Box Brownie Mix
- 1 Package Cream Cheese
- 2 Egg
- 1/2 Cup Oil
- 1 Can Pie Filling, Blueberry
- 1/2 Cup Sugar
- 1 Tsp Vanilla
- 1/4 Cup Water, Warm

Directions:

1. Combine all brownie ingredients and mix. In a separate bowl, combine cream cheese, sugar, egg and vanilla and mix until smooth. Grease skillets and pour in brownie batter. Top with cheesecake and cherry pie filling, using a knife to blend to give it that marbled look.

2. Supply your smoker with wood pellets and follow the start-up procedure. Preheat the grill, with the lid closed, to 350°F and bake for about 30 minutes.

3. Let cool for about 10 minutes and enjoy!

Ultimate Baked Garlic Bread

Servings: 4

Cooking Time: 20 Minutes

Ingredients:

- 1 baguette
- 1/2 Cup softened butter
- 1/2 Cup mayonnaise
- 4 Tablespoon chopped Italian parsley
- 6 Clove garlic, minced
- salt
- chile flakes
- 1 Cup mozzarella cheese
- 1/2 Cup Parmesan cheese

Directions:

1. Supply your smoker with wood pellets and follow the start-up procedure. Preheat the grill, with the lid closed, to 375° F.

2. Lay baguette on a cutting board and cut it in half lengthwise.

3. In a bowl, add butter, mayonnaise, parsley, garlic, salt and chile flakes. Mix well.

4. Spread butter mixture on baguette halves and top with mozzarella and Parmesan cheese.

5. Place baguette on the grill (if you like the bread crisp, do not use foil and if you like it soft, wrap with foil). Grill for approximately 15 to 25 minutes. Serve warm. Enjoy! Grill: 375 ˚F

Baked Wood-fired Pizza

Servings: 6

Cooking Time: 12 Minutes

Ingredients:

- 2/3 Cup warm water (110°F to 115°F)
- 2 1/2 Teaspoon active dry yeast
- 1/2 Teaspoon granulated sugar
- 1 Teaspoon kosher salt
- 1 Tablespoon oil
- 2 Cup all-purpose flour
- 1/4 Cup fine cornmeal
- 1 Large grilled portobello mushroom, sliced
- 1 Jar pickled artichoke hearts, drained and chopped
- 1 Cup shredded fontina cheese
- 1/2 Cup shaved Parmigiano-Reggiano cheese, divided
- To Taste Roasted Garlic, minced
- 1/4 Cup extra-virgin olive oil
- To Taste banana peppers

Directions:

1. In a glass bowl, stir together the warm water, yeast and sugar. Let stand until the mixture starts to foam, about 10 minutes. In a mixer, combine 1-3/4 cup flour, sugar and salt. Stir oil into the yeast mixture. Slowly add the liquid to the dry ingredients while slowly increasing the mixers speed until fully combined. The dough should be smooth and not sticky.

2. Knead the dough on a floured surface, gradually adding the remaining flour as needed to prevent the dough from sticking, until smooth, about 5 to 10 minutes.

3. Form the dough into a ball. Apply a thin layer of olive oil to a large bowl. Place the dough into the bowl and coat the dough ball with a small amount of olive oil. Cover and let rise in a warm place for about 1 hour or until doubled in size.

4. When ready to cook, set smoker temperature to 450°F and preheat, lid closed for 15 minutes.

5. Place a pizza stone in the grill while it preheats.

6. Punch the dough down and roll it out into a 12-inch circle on a floured surface.

7. Spread the cornmeal evenly on the pizza peel. Place the dough on the pizza peel and assemble the toppings evenly in the following order: olive oil, roasted garlic, fontina, portobello, artichoke hearts, Parmigiano-Reggiano and banana peppers.

8. Carefully slide the assembled pizza from the pizza peel to the preheated pizza stone and bake until the crust is golden brown, about 10 to 12 minutes. Enjoy!

Smoky Apple Crepes

Servings: 6   Cooking Time: 60 Minutes

Ingredients:

- 1/2 Cup Apple Juice
- 2 Lbs Apples
- 2 Tbsp Brown Sugar
- 5 Tbsp Butter
- 3 Tbsp Butter, Melted
- Tt Caramel
- 3/4 Tsp Cinnamon, Ground
- Tt Cinnamon-Sugar
- 3/4 Tsp Cornstarch
- 2 Eggs
- 1 Cup Flour
- 2 Tsp Lemon Juice
- Tennessee Apple Butter Seasoning
- 1/2 Cup Water
- 3/4 Cup Milk

Directions:

1. Supply your smoker with wood pellets and follow the start-up procedure. Preheat the grill, with the lid closed, to 225° F. If using a gas or charcoal grill, set it up for low, indirect heat.

2. Peel, halve, and core apples.

3. Season apples with Tennessee Apple Butter then place directly on the grill grate, and smoke for 1 hour.

4. Meanwhile, prepare crêpe batter: combine eggs, milk, water, flour, and 3 tbsp of melted butter in a blender, and blend until smooth.

5. Refrigerate for 30 minutes.

6. Remove apples from grill, cool slightly, then slice thin.

7. Place a cast iron skillet on the grill and melt 3 tbsp butter with brown sugar, cinnamon, cornstarch, apple and lemon juices. Cook for 5 minutes until thick.

8. Add apples and cook for another 3 to 5 minutes, stirring to coat apples in sauce.

9. Remove from grill and set aside.

10. Preheat griddle to medium-low. If using a standard grill, preheat a cast iron skillet on medium-low heat.

11. Melt 1 teaspoon of butter on the griddle.

12. Then add ½ cup of batter, and spread with the bottom of a metal spatula, working quickly, as the batter cooks fast.

13. Cook one minute per side, until edges begin to brown. Remove from griddle, set aside, and repeat with remaining batter.

14. Spoon ¼ cup of apple filling into the center of each crêpe, then quarter-fold into a triangle.

15. Serve warm with additional apple filling, drizzle of warm caramel, and a dusting of cinnamon-sugar.

Smoked Lemon Tea

Servings: 6 - 8

Cooking Time: 60 Minutes

Ingredients:

- 8 Black Tea Bags
- 4 Cups Boiling Water
- 2 Cups Ice
- 8 Lemons
- 2 Cups Sugar
- 2 Cups Water

Directions:

1. Place the tea bags in a heat-safe pitcher. Bring 4 Cups of water to a boil and pour over tea bags. Let steep for 5-10 minutes. Remove tea bags and set pitcher aside to cool.

2. Turn on your grill and set to smoke mode. Combine 2 cups of sugar and 2 cups water in a small aluminum pan. Smoke for about 45 minutes, stirring occasionally, or until the mixture reduces to a thick, simple syrup. Remove from the grill and let it cool.

3. Supply your smoker with wood pellets and follow the start-up procedure. Preheat the grill, with the lid closed, to 450° F. If using a charcoal or gas grill, set heat to high.

4. Cut the lemons in half and sear over the flame broiler until charred, about 7 minutes. Remove from grill and set aside to cool.

5. Juice the lemons into a medium bowl. Pour lemon juice through a metal strainer into the tea pitcher to remove seeds and pulp.

6. Pour the cooled simple syrup into pitcher and stir until fully incorporated with tea and lemons. Add 2 cups of ice and refrigerate until serving.

Lemon Strawberry Rhubarb Pie

Servings: 8

Cooking Time: 30 Minutes

Ingredients:

- 1/3 Cup Flour
- 1 Tbsp Lemon, Zest
- 1 Prepard Pie Shell, Deep
- 3 Stalks Rhubarb
- 2 1/2 Cups Strawberry
- 1 Cup Sugar

Directions:

1. Summer baking never has to stop when you can use your Wood Pellet Grill to bake anything from cookies to pie! In this recipe, we will show you how to bake a delicious barbecued strawberry rhubarb pie without turning your kitchen into an oven.

2. Supply your smoker with wood pellets and follow the start-up procedure. Preheat the grill, with the lid closed, to 400° F.

3. Slice rhubarb and strawberries into bite sized pieces. Combine sugar, flour and lemon zest with rhubarb and strawberries. Pour into prepared pie crust. Cover with top crust.

4. Bake in Grill for 1 hour or until crust is crispy.

5. Serve hot.

Donut Bread Pudding

Servings: 8

Cooking Time: 40 Minutes

Ingredients:

- 16 Cake Donuts
- 1/2 Cup Raisins, seedless
- 5 eggs
- 3/4 Cup sugar
- 2 Cup heavy cream
- 2 Teaspoon vanilla extract
- 1 Teaspoon ground cinnamon
- 3/4 Cup Butter, melted, cooled slightly
- Ice Cream

Directions:

1. Lightly butter a 9- by 13-inch baking pan. Layer the donuts in an even thickness in the pan. Distribute the raisins over the top, if using. Drizzle evenly with the butter.

2. Make the custard: In a medium bowl, whisk together the sugar, eggs, cream, vanilla, and cinnamon. Whisk in the butter. Pour over the donuts. Let sit for 10 to 15 minutes, periodically pushing the donuts down into the custard. Cover with foil.

3. Supply your smoker with wood pellets and follow the start-up procedure. Preheat the grill, with the lid closed, to 350° F.

4. Bake the bread pudding for 30 to 40 minutes, or until the custard is set. Remove the foil and continue to bake for 10 additional minutes to lightly brown the top. Grill: 350 ℉

5. Let cool slightly before cutting into squares. Drizzle with melted ice cream, if desired. Enjoy!

PORK RECIPES

Holiday Smoked Cheese Log

Servings: 8

Cooking Time: 60 Minutes

Ingredients:

- 16 Ounce cream cheese
- 3 Cup shredded cheddar cheese
- 1 Tablespoon Worcestershire sauce
- 1 Teaspoon hot sauce
- 8 Slices bacon
- 2 green onion
- 1 Cup coarsely chopped pecans

Directions:

1. In a mixing bowl, using an electric mixer or large spoon, combine the cream cheese (room temperature) and the cheddar cheese.

2. Add in the Worcestershire sauce and hot sauce. Mix again.

3. Add in the cooked and crumbled bacon and chopped green onions. Mix until combined.

4. Cover the bowl with plastic wrap and refrigerate for 4 hours or until the cheese mixture is firm enough to mold. Shape it into a log and layer the outside with the toasted pecans.

5. Cover with plastic wrap. Freeze the cheese log overnight to make sure it doesn't get too soft while it's smoking.

6. The next day supply your smoker with wood pellets and follow the start-up procedure. Preheat the grill, with the lid closed, to 180° F.

7. Take the cheese log out of the freezer and unwrap. Place on a cooking sheet and smoke for 1 hour. Keep an eye on it to make sure it doesn't get too soft. Grill: 180 °F

8. Move the cheese log to a serving tray and serve with your favorite crackers. (If the cheese is too soft, throw it in the fridge for an hour or two.)

St. Louis Bbq Ribs

Servings: 4

Cooking Time: 240 Minutes

Ingredients:

- 2 Rack St. Louis-style ribs
- 1/4 Cup Pork & Poultry Rub
- 1 Cup apple juice
- 1 Bottle Sweet & Heat BBQ Sauce

Directions:

1. Trim ribs and peel off membrane from the back of ribs. Apply an even coat of rub to the front and back of ribs. Let sit for 20 minutes and up to 4 hours if refrigerated.

2. Supply your smoker with wood pellets and follow the start-up procedure. Preheat the grill, with the lid closed, to 225° F.

3. Place ribs bone side down on grill grate. Put apple juice in a spray bottle and evenly spray ribs. Grill: 225 °F

4. After 3 hours, remove ribs from grill and wrap them in aluminum foil. Leave an opening at one end, pour in remainder of apple juice (about 6 oz) into the foil and wrap tightly.

5. Place ribs back on grill, meat side down and smoke for an additional 3 hours. Grill: 225 °F Probe: 203 °F

6. After 1 hour, start checking the internal temperature of ribs. Ribs are done when the internal temperature reaches 203°F. Grill: 225 °F

7. When ribs are done, remove from the foil and brush a light layer of sauce on the front and back on the ribs.

8. Return to the grill and cook an additional 10 minutes to set the sauce. Grill: 225 °F

9. After sauce has set, take ribs off the grill and let rest for 10 minutes. To serve, slice ribs in between the bones. Enjoy!

Egg Bacon French Toast Panini

Servings: 2

Cooking Time: 10 Minutes

Ingredients:

- ➢ 6 Bacon Slices
- ➢ 1 Tbsp Black Pepper
- ➢ 4 Brioche Sandwich Slices, Day Old
- ➢ 2 Tbsp Butter
- ➢ 1 Tbsp Cinnamon-Sugar
- ➢ 6 Eggs
- ➢ 1 Tbsp Heavy Cream
- ➢ 1 Tbsp Maple Syrup
- ➢ 1 Tbsp Salt

Directions:

1. Supply your smoker with wood pellets and follow the start-up procedure. Preheat the grill, with the lid open, to 375° F. If using a gas or charcoal grill, set heat to medium heat. For all other grills, preheat cast iron skillet on grill grates.

2. Place butter on griddle and spread to coat surface.

3. In a pie plate, whisk together 2 eggs, heavy cream, and maple syrup.

4. Soak both sides of bread slices in egg mixture and transfer to griddle. Cook for 2 minutes, flipping halfway until egg mixture is cooked and golden. Set aside.

5. Lay bacon on the griddle, and cook 3 minutes per side, until golden.

6. Transfer to lower right-hand corner of griddle to keep warm.

7. Crack 4 eggs on top of rendered bacon fat. Season with salt and pepper. Cook 1 minute per side, or to desired doneness.

8. Lay eggs on top of French toast, add bacon, then place the other slice of French Toast on top.

9. Transfer back to griddle for another minute to warm, sprinkle with extra cinnamon-sugar, then slice in half and serve hot.

Pork & Pepperoni Burgers

Servings: 4

Cooking Time: 60 Minutes

Ingredients:

- ➢ 1lb (450g) bulk pork sausage, preferably Italian
- ➢ 1lb (450g) ground pork, well chilled
- ➢ 8 slices of bacon, preferably thick-cut
- ➢ 8oz (225g) grated mozzarella cheese, plus more
- ➢ 1 tsp Italian seasoning
- ➢ ½ cup pizza sauce
- ➢ 1½oz (40g) pepperoni, roughly chopped

Directions:

1. Wet your hands with cold water. In a large bowl, combine the sausage and ground pork until well mixed. Line a rimmed sheet pan with aluminum foil. Divide the meat into 4 equal-sized balls and place on the sheet pan. Spray the lower third of a soda can (including the bottom) with cooking spray. Firmly press the can into one of the meatballs to create a meat bowl with uniform sides. Gently twist or rock the can to remove. Use your hands to repair any cracks in the bowl.

2. Wrap 2 slices of bacon around the circumference of the bowl and secure with toothpicks. Repeat with the remaining meatballs, respraying the can with cooking spray as necessary. Chill for 1 hour.

3. Supply your smoker with wood pellets and follow the start-up procedure. Preheat the grill, with the lid closed, to 300° F.

4. Place the patties cup side up on the grate and grill for 30 minutes. Use paper towels to blot any grease that pools at the bottom of the cups.

5. Sprinkle 2 tablespoons of cheese into each cup. Top each patty with equal amounts of Italian seasoning, pizza sauce, and pepperoni. Generously sprinkle more cheese over the top. Continue to grill until the bacon crisps, the cheese melts, and the internal temperature reaches 160°F (71°C), about 20 to 30 minutes more.

6. Remove the burgers from the grill and rest for 3 minutes. Remove the toothpicks and serve immediately.

Smoked Pork Tomato Tamales

Servings: 6-8	Cooking Time: 60 Minutes

Ingredients:

- 1 Boneless, Netted Pork Roast
- 1 Cup, Fresh Cilantro, Chopped
- 3 Cloves Garlic, Peeled
- 20 Dried Cornhusks
- 1 Tbsp Lime Juice
- ¼ Cup Olive Oil
- 1 Onion, Quartered
- 4 - 6 Cups Prepared Masa Harina Tamale Dough
- 3 – 4 Serrano Peppers, Deseeded
- 1 Tbsp Sweet Heat Rub
- 1 Lb. Tomatillos, Husked And Washed

Directions:

1. Began by soaking the corn husks in a pan filled with water. Soak for 2 – 4 hours, or if needed, overnight.

2. Unwrap the tomatillos from their shell and place all of them into a grill basket followed by a few Serranos, deseeded, garlic cloves and 1 onion cut into quarters.

3. Supply your smoker with wood pellets and follow the start-up procedure. Preheat the grill, with the lid open, to 400° F. If you're using a gas or charcoal grill, set it up for medium low heat, and use smoke chips to fill your grill with smoke for 15 minutes. Place the grill basket filled with your vegetables and roast them over an open flame on your smoker until vegetables have become charred.

4. Place tomatillos, peppers, garlic and onions in a bowl, cover with plastic wrap, and let stand until cool enough to handle, 10 to 15 minutes.

5. Season the pork roast generously with Sweet Heat Rub and grill at 350°F for 1 hour until the roast has a nice crust on the outside.

6. While the pork roast is cooking, add a handful of cilantro, charred vegetables, 1 tbsp of Sweet Heat Rub, 1 tbsp lime juice, and ¼ cup of olive oil to a food processor. Pulse in food processor until mixture is consistent. Set aside

7. After the pork roast has been grilled for an hour, turn heat down to 275°F. Put roast in pan with about a cup of water, cover with aluminum foil and cook for another 4 hours or until the roast can be shredded. Pour chile verde sauce over shredded pork and toss to combine.

8. To being assembling tamales, place a corn husk on a work surface. Place 2-3 tablespoons of tamale dough on larger end of husk and spread into a rectangle, about ¼" thick, leaving a small border along the edge. Place large tablespoon of chili and pork filling on top of dough. Fold over sides of husk so dough

surrounds filling, then fold bottom of husk up and secure closed by tying a thin strip of husk around tamale.

9. To cook tamales, place them in a large metal colander over a large stockpot filled with water. Cover and let steam for 1 hour. After the tamales have been steamed, take them off and grill them at 350°F for about 10-20 minutes until corn husks have charred marks.

Grilled Bacon Dog

Servings: 4

Cooking Time: 25 Minutes

Ingredients:

- 16 hot dogs
- 16 Slices Bacon, sliced
- 2 Vidalia onion, sliced
- 16 hot dog buns
- 'Que BBQ Sauce
- Velveeta cheese

Directions:

1. Supply your smoker with wood pellets and follow the start-up procedure. Preheat the grill, with the lid closed, to 375° F.

2. Wrap bacon strips around the hot dogs, and grill directly on the grill grate for 10 minutes each side. Grill onions at the same time as the hot dogs, and cook for 10 -15 minutes.

3. Open hot dog buns and spread Traeger 'Que sauce, the grilled hot dogs, cheese sauce and grilled onions. Top with vegetables. Serve, enjoy!

Savory Pork Belly Banh Mi

Servings: 4

Cooking Time: 420 Minutes

Ingredients:

- 2 Carrots, Sliced
- 1 Tbsp Cilantro, Minced
- 1 Tbsp Honey
- 2 Kirby Cucumbers, Sliced Thin
- 1 Lime, Zest & Juice
- 2 Tbsp Pickling Spice
- 1 Tbsp Ponzu
- 2 Lbs Pork Belly
- 1 Cup Rice Wine Vinegar
- 2 Tbsp Salt
- 4 Sandwich Buns
- 1 Small Daikon Radish, Sliced Thin
- To Taste, Smoky Salt & Cracked Pepper Rub
- 2 Tbsp Soy Sauce
- 1/2 Cup Sriracha Hot Sauce
- 4 Cloves Star Anise
- 1/2 Cup Sugar
- 1 Cup Water

Directions:

1. 30 minutes before you plan to put the belly on the smoker season liberally with the Smoky Salt and Cracked Pepper rub.

2. Supply your smoker with wood pellets and follow the start-up procedure. Preheat the grill, with the lid open, to 240° F. If using a gas or charcoal grill, set it up for low, indirect heat.

3. Place the belly on the smoker with a tin pan underneath the meat to catch the drippings. Smoke for 7 hours or until you reach an internal temp of 195 degrees. Remove the pork and let rest for 30 minutes.

4. Make the homemade pickles: Place pickling spice and star anise in a small sauce pan and toast. Once fragrant add vinegar and bring to a boil, cook for 3 minutes. Add the water, sugar, and salt and return to a boil, cook for 5 minutes. Strain the liquid and immediately pour over the vegetables, making sure the vegetables are submerged. Set in the fridge once cool.

5. Make the Sriracha Lime Sauce: Combine the sriracha, lime, soy sauce, honey, cilantro and ponzu in a mixing bowl and whisk until combined.

6. Assemble the sandwiches, placing sliced pork belly and homemade pickles on a roll before topping it with the sriracha lime sauce.

Game Day Cheese Dip

Servings: 6

Cooking Time: 18 Minutes

Ingredients:

- 8 Slices bacon
- 8 cream cheese, softened
- 1/2 Cup mayonnaise
- 2 Teaspoon Dijon mustard
- 1 3/4 Cup Swiss cheese
- 3 scallions, chopped
- 2 Teaspoon Horseradish, fresh

Directions:

1. Supply your smoker with wood pellets and follow the start-up procedure. Preheat the grill, with the lid closed, to 400° F.

2. In a mixing bowl, combine cream cheese, mayonnaise, dijon mustard, swiss cheese (except cheese for topping), scallions, horseradish and crumbled bacon.

3. Transfer to a shallow small casserole or baking dish. Top the dip with the additional 1/4 cup of extra swiss cheese.

4. Place the casserole dish on the Traeger grill grate and cook until golden and bubbly at edges, 15 to 18 minutes. Grill: 400 ˚F

5. Top with chopped scallions. Enjoy!

Baked Bacon Caramel Popcorn

Servings: 6

Cooking Time: 30 Minutes

Ingredients:

- 1 Pound bacon
- 1 Cup popcorn kernels
- 2 Stick unsalted butter
- 1/2 Teaspoon salt
- 2 Cup brown sugar, packed
- 1/4 Cup Kentucky bourbon
- 11 Teaspoon baking soda
- 2 Teaspoon vanilla

Directions:

1. Supply your smoker with wood pellets and follow the start-up procedure. Preheat the grill, with the lid closed, to 350° F.

2. Lay bacon strips directly on the grill grate and cook for 15 to 20 minutes or until fat is rendered and bacon is lightly browned. Remove from grill and chop into 1/2 inch pieces. Set aside. Grill: 350 ˚F

3. While grill is cooling, pop kernels in a popcorn maker. Place popped kernels and bacon in a large bowl and set aside.

4. In a medium saucepan over medium-high heat, combine butter, salt and sugar. Bring the mixture to a boil and cook until an instant-read thermometer reads 275°F. Immediately remove from heat and whisk in bourbon, vanilla and baking powder. Use caution because it will bubble up and release steam.

5. Reduce grill temperature to 225°F and let cool for 10 to 15 minutes. Grill: 225 ˚F

6. Pour caramel sauce over bacon and popcorn and toss to coat. Spread popcorn out onto a large sheet tray lined with a piece of parchment paper.

7. Place sheet tray directly on the grill grate and cook at 225°F for 15 to 20 minutes, watching closely to make sure the caramel doesn't burn. Grill: 225 ˚F

8. Remove from grill and pour popcorn on a counter lined with parchment paper. Let cool 30 minutes or until caramel has set. Enjoy!

Egg Sausage Casserole

Servings: 12

Cooking Time: 60 Minutes

Ingredients:

- 12 sausage links
- 30 oz hash browns, thawed
- 1 1/2 c. marble jack cheese, shredded
- 1/2 tsp pepper
- 12 large eggs
- 1 tsp salt
- 1/2 c. yellow onion, chopped
- 1 c. milk

Directions:

1. Supply your smoker with wood pellets and follow the start-up procedure. Preheat the grill, with the lid closed, to 350° F.

2. Grill sausage links on the preheated grill for 10-15 minutes or until heated through.

3. Remove the sausage links from grill and cut them into 1-inch pieces.

4. Spray a 9" ×13" tin pan with non-stick spray. Spread out hash browns on bottom of pan. Top with sausage pieces.

5. Combine eggs, salt, pepper, 1 c. cheese, onions, and milk in a bowl. Pour the mixture over sausage and hash browns. Then top with the remaining 1/2 c. of cheese.

6. Transfer the tin pan to the grill grate, and grill at 350 °F for 45 minutes or until the middle is set.

Smoked Pork Loin With Sauerkraut And Apples

Servings: 4

Cooking Time: 120 Minutes

Ingredients:

- 1 (2 to 2-1/2 lb) pork loin roast
- Pork & Poultry Rub
- 1 Pound sauerkraut
- 2 Large cooking apples, peeled, cored and sliced
- 1 Large sweet onion, thinly sliced
- 1/3 Cup brown sugar
- 1 Cup dark beer
- 2 Tablespoon butter
- 2 Whole bay leaves

Directions:

1. Supply your smoker with wood pellets and follow the start-up procedure. Preheat the grill, with the lid closed, to 180° F.

2. Season the pork loin on all sides with Traeger Pork & Poultry Rub or salt and pepper. Place the roast directly on the grill grate, close the lid, and smoke for 1 hour. Grill: 180 °F

3. In a large Dutch oven or glass baking dish, layer the sauerkraut, apples, onions, brown sugar, beer, butter and bay leaves. Lay the smoked pork loin directly on top of the sauerkraut mixture. Top the pan with a lid or a layer of foil.

4. Increase Traeger temperature to 350°F, and return the pan to the grill. Close the lid and roast the pork for an additional hour, or until the internal temperature on an instant-read meat thermometer reads 160°F. Grill: 350 °F Probe: 160 °F

5. Transfer the roast to a cutting board and let it rest. Meanwhile, gently stir the sauerkraut mixture and arrange on a serving platter. Slice the pork roast and layer on the sauerkraut and apples. Enjoy!

Grilled St. Louis Style Ribs With Tequila Bbq

Ingredients:

- 1/2 Cup Brown Sugar
- 2 Garlic, Cloves
- 3 Tbsp Honey
- 1 Cup Ketchup
- 1/2 Squeezed Lime
- 3 Tbsp Molasses
- 1 Jar Mustard
- 2 Slabs Slabs St. Louis-Style Rib Racks
- 1 Bottle Sweet Heat Rub
- 1/4 Cup Tequila Blanco

Directions:

1. First, make the barbecue sauce. In a mixing bowl, add the ketchup, brown sugar, garlic cloves, molasses, honey, tequila, lime, and 1 tbsp Sweet Heat Rub. Mix together well until glaze is blended together. Set aside.

2. Prepare the ribs. Pat the ribs dry with paper towels, then pull the thin membrane off the back of the ribs and discard. Using a basting brush, coat the meat on both sides with a thin layer of mustard and season heavily with Sweet Heat Rub until the ribs are completely coated. Repeat with the second rack of ribs. Place the ribs on a baking sheet and refrigerate overnight, or for 12 hours if you choose to.

3. Once the ribs have finished marinating, remove them from the refrigerator and set out two sheets of large, heavy duty aluminum foil. Place one rack of ribs on each sheet of foil, meat-side down, and fold the edges over to form a sealed pouch.

4. Supply your smoker with wood pellets and follow the start-up procedure. Preheat the grill, with the lid open, to 225° F. If you're using a gas or charcoal grill, set it up for low, indirect heat. Place the rib packets on the grill, meat-side up, and smoke for 2-3 hours, or until the ribs are nearly tender.

5. Remove the ribs from the grill and take the aluminum foil off the ribs and place them back onto the grill for another hour. Brush generously with the tequila barbecue sauce on both sides, then grill for 5 minutes, meat- side up. Baste the ribs one more time with the barbecue sauce, then flip them meat-side down and grill for a final 5 minutes. The ribs should be sticky and caramelized. Remove the ribs from the grill and serve immediately with the remaining barbecue sauce.

Bbq Rib Sandwich

Servings: 2

Cooking Time: 180 Minutes

Ingredients:

- 3 Rack baby back pork ribs
- cracked black pepper
- kosher salt
- 1 Cup 'Que BBQ Sauce
- 4 hoagie rolls
- 1 Jar Pickles
- 1 yellow onion, thinly sliced

Directions:

1. Peel membrane from back side of the ribs. Lightly season with cracked black pepper and salt.

2. Supply your smoker with wood pellets and follow the start-up procedure. Preheat the grill, with the lid closed, to 225° F.

3. Cook meaty side up for two hours, then flip the ribs to meaty side down and cook for one more hour. Grill: 225 ˚F

4. Remove ribs from grill and flip over so they are laying bone side up on a cutting board. Using a sharp knife, cut down the center of each bone and remove bones using your fingers.

5. Flip ribs back over and brush with half of the Traeger 'Que BBQ Sauce. Place back on the grill for 5-10 minutes to set the sauce. Remove from the grill and set aside.

6. Cut rib racks to match the length of the hoagie rolls. Split the hoagie rolls in half and place ribs on the bottom bun.

7. Top with pickles, onions, more BBQ sauce and top bun. Enjoy!

Korean Pulled Pork Lettuce Wraps

Servings: 8   Cooking Time: 480 Minutes

Ingredients:

- 1 bone-in pork shoulder, about 6lb (2.7kg)
- 1 cup low-carb beer or sugar-free light-colored soda
- for the sauce
- 1½ cups low-carb barbecue sauce
- ¼ cup low-carb beer or sugar-free light- or dark-colored soda
- 3 tbsp gochujang
- 3 tbsp light soy sauce
- 1 tbsp rice wine vinegar
- 1 tbsp toasted Asian sesame oil
- 1 tsp gochugaru
- for the rub
- 3 tbsp coarse salt
- 3 tbsp gochugaru
- 3 tbsp granulated light brown sugar or low-carb substitute
- 2 tsp granulated garlic
- 2 tsp onion powder
- 1 tsp ground ginger

Directions:

1. Supply your smoker with wood pellets and follow the start-up procedure. Preheat the grill, with the lid closed, to 250° F.

2. In a small bowl, make the barbecue sauce by whisking together the ingredients. Cover and refrigerate until ready to serve.

3. In a small bowl, make the rub by combining the ingredients. Rinse the meat with cold running water and pat dry with paper towels. Sprinkle the rub evenly over the surface, using your fingertips to pat it on.

4. Place the pork shoulder on the grate and smoke until the internal temperature reaches 165°F (74°C), about 4 to 5 hours. Transfer the meat to an aluminum foil roasting pan. Add the beer and then cover the pan tightly with heavy-duty aluminum foil. Continue to cook until the internal temperature reaches 200°F (93°C), about 3 hours more. (Keep the probe from touching bone or it will give you a false reading.) When the pork is tender enough to pull, the meat will release easily from the bone.

5. Transfer the pork shoulder to a cutting board. Drain the accumulated juices into a separate container and reserve. While the pork is still hot, pull out the bone and separate the meat into chunks. Using meat claws, forks, or your fingers, pull the meat into shreds, discarding any lumps of fat or undesirable bits. Return the meat to the pan. Stir in some of the reserved cooking juices if desired. You want the pork to be moist but not soupy.

6. Wrap the hot pork in lettuce leaves. Top with thinly sliced garlic, thinly sliced crosswise jalapeños, toasted sesame seeds, pickled ginger, and barbecue sauce. You can also serve the pork the American way: piled high on sesame seed buns.

VEGETABLES RECIPES

Smoked Mashed Potatoes

Servings: 6

Cooking Time: 45 Minutes

Ingredients:

- 2 Pound red bliss potatoes, washed and diced medium
- chicken stock or water
- 1/2 Stick salted butter
- 1 Cup whole milk
- 1/2 Cup sour cream
- 1/2 Cup shredded or grated Parmesan cheese
- kosher salt
- freshly ground black pepper
- 1/2 Cup fresh sliced green onions

Directions:

1. Place the diced red potatoes into a small saucepan or stockpot and cover with chicken stock or water.

2. Bring to a boil and cook on a simmer until fork tender, then cook 4 to 5 minutes past that until soft.

3. Supply your smoker with wood pellets and follow the start-up procedure. Preheat the grill, with the lid closed, to 400° F.

4. In a separate ovenproof pan, such as a cast iron skillet, add butter and milk and place in the Traeger during start up, until melted (approximately 7 to 10 minutes). Grill: 400 °F

5. Carefully remove the butter/milk mixture from the Traeger using heatproof gloves.

6. Drain the potatoes and place into a large bowl. Add the melted butter/milk mixture and slowly mash.

7. Add sour cream, cheese and green onions, then season to taste with salt and pepper.

8. Place into the cast iron skillet, then place the skillet back into the Traeger and cook until the potatoes have a slight crust and are bubbling, about 15 minutes. Grill: 400 °F

9. Carefully remove the mashed potatoes from the Traeger using heatproof gloves. Allow to cool for 5 minutes. Scoop and enjoy!

Roasted Hasselback Potatoes By Doug Scheiding

Servings: 6

Cooking Time: 120 Minutes

Ingredients:

- ➢ 6 Large russet potatoes
- ➢ 1 Pound bacon
- ➢ 1/2 Cup butter
- ➢ salt
- ➢ black pepper
- ➢ 1 Cup cheddar cheese
- ➢ 3 Whole scallions

Directions:

1. To cut potatoes, place two wooden spoons on either side of the potato (this prevents your knife from going all the way through). Slice potato into thin chips leaving about 1/4" attached on the bottom.

2. Freeze bacon slices for about 30 minutes then cut into small pieces about the size of a stamp. Place these in the cracks between every other slice.

3. Place the potato in a large cast iron skillet. Top the potato with slices of hard butter (you can also place thin slivers of cold butter between the potato slices with the bacon if desired). Season with salt and pepper.

4. Supply your smoker with wood pellets and follow the start-up procedure. Preheat the grill, with the lid closed, to 350° F.

5. Place the cast iron directly on the grill grate and cook for two hours. Top potatoes with more butter and baste with melted butter every 30 minutes.

6. In the last 10 minutes of cooking, sprinkle with cheddar and return to grill to melt.

7. To finish, top with chives or scallions. Enjoy!

Grilled Asparagus And Hollandaise Sauce

Servings: 4

Cooking Time: 10 Minutes

Ingredients:

➢ 1 Pound asparagus

➢ 2 Teaspoon red pepper flakes

➢ 2 Tablespoon olive oil

➢ salt and pepper

➢ 4 egg yolk

➢ 1 Tablespoon lemon juice

➢ 1/2 Cup butter, melted

➢ cayenne pepper

➢ salt

Directions:

1. Supply your smoker with wood pellets and follow the start-up procedure. Preheat the grill, with the lid closed, to 375° F.

2. In a large bowl, mix asparagus with olive oil, red pepper flakes and salt. Arrange asparagus on a cooking sheet and take to the grill. Cook for approximately 10 to 15 minutes. Grill: 375 ℉

3. In an aluminum bowl, whisk the egg yolks well. Add the lemon juice and whisk until creamy.

4. Place bowl over a double boiler, over low heat, making sure that it does not touches the water.

5. While whisking, add the melted butter slowly. Whisk until it doubles the volume. Take off the heat, still whisking and add the cayenne pepper and salt.

6. Arrange asparagus over a serving plater. Pour hollandaise sauce over asparagus and serve. Enjoy!

Baked Heirloom Tomato Tart

Servings: 4

Cooking Time: 45 Minutes

Ingredients:

- ➤ 1 Whole Puff Pastry Sheet
- ➤ 2 Pound heirloom tomatoes, various shapes and sizes
- ➤ 1/2 Tablespoon kosher salt
- ➤ 1/2 Cup Ricotta Cheese
- ➤ 5 Whole eggs
- ➤ 1 To Taste salt and pepper
- ➤ 1/2 Teaspoon thyme leaves
- ➤ 1/2 Teaspoon red pepper flakes
- ➤ 4 Sprig thyme

Directions:

1. Supply your smoker with wood pellets and follow the start-up procedure. Preheat the grill, with the lid closed, to 350° F.

2. Place the puff pastry on a parchment lined sheet tray, and make a cut ¾ of the way through the pastry, ½" from the edge.

3. Slice the tomatoes and season with salt. Place on a sheet tray lined with paper towels.

4. In a small bowl combine the ricotta, 4 of the eggs, salt, thyme leaves, red pepper flakes and black pepper. Whisk together until combined. Spread the ricotta mixture over the puff pastry, staying within ½" from the edge.

5. In a small bowl whisk the last egg. Brush the egg wash onto the exposed edges of the pastry.

6. Place the sheet tray directly on the grill grate and bake for 45 minutes, rotating half-way through. Grill: 350 °F

7. When the edges are browned and the moisture from the tomatoes has evaporated, remove from the grill and let cool 5-7 minutes before serving. Enjoy!

Sweet Potato Marshmallow Casserole

Servings: 6

Cooking Time: 60 Minutes

Ingredients:

- ➢ 5 Yams
- ➢ 1 1/2 Stick butter
- ➢ 1/2 Cup brown sugar
- ➢ 1 Teaspoon vanilla
- ➢ 1 Teaspoon kosher salt
- ➢ 1 Teaspoon cracked black pepper
- ➢ 1 Marshmallows, miniature
- ➢ 1/4 Unsalted Butter, Softened

Directions:

1. Supply your smoker with wood pellets and follow the start-up procedure. Preheat the grill, with the lid closed, to 375° F.

2. Pierce the skin of the yams with a fork a few times. Place on a baking sheet or foil tin inside the grill and let roast for 50 minutes or until extremely softened. Grill: 375 ˚F

3. Remove yams from the grill and set aside until cool enough to handle. While the potatoes cool, with a stiff whisk, whip together 1/2 cup softened butter, the brown sugar, vanilla, salt and pepper.

4. Remove and discard skins from sweet potatoes and mash until smooth. Fold in the butter mixture and transfer to a cast iron pan.

5. Place cast iron on the grill and bake for 15-20 minutes. Remove from the grill, top with marshmallows and dot with remaining 1/4 cup butter.

6. Place back in the grill for 15 minutes until warm and the marshmallows are golden. Enjoy! Grill: 375 ˚F

Double-smoked Cheese Potatoes

Servings: 12

Cooking Time: 35 Minutes

Ingredients:

➢ 4 large baking potatoes (12 to 14 ounces each—preferably organic)

➢ 1 1/2 tablespoons bacon fat or butter, melted, or extra virgin olive oil

➢ Coarse salt (sea or kosher) and freshly ground black pepper

➢ 4 strips artisanal bacon (like Nueske's), cut crosswise into 1/4-inch slivers

➢ 6 tablespoons (3/4 stick) cold unsalted butter, thinly sliced

➢ 2 scallions, trimmed, white and green parts finely chopped (about 4 tablespoons)

➢ 2 cups coarsely grated smoked or regular white cheddar cheese (about 8 ounces)

➢ 1/2 cup sour cream

➢ Spanish smoked paprika (pimentón) or sweet paprika, for sprinkling

Directions:

1. Supply your smoker with wood pellets and follow the start-up procedure. Preheat the grill, with the lid closed, to 400° F.Add enough wood for 1 hour of smoking as specified by the manufacturer.

2. Scrub the potatoes on all sides with a vegetable brush. Rinse well under cold running water and blot dry with paper towels. Prick each potato several times with a fork (this keeps the spud from exploding and facilitates the smoke absorption). Brush or rub the potato on all sides with the bacon fat and season generously with salt and pepper.

3. Place the potatoes on the smoker rack. Smoke until the skins are crisp and the potatoes are tender in the center (they'll be easy to pierce with a slender metal skewer), about 1 hour.

4. Meanwhile, place the bacon in a cold skillet and fry over medium heat until browned and crisp, 3 to 4 minutes. Drain off the bacon fat (save the fat for future potatoes).

5. Transfer the potatoes to a cutting board and let cool slightly. Cut each potato in half lengthwise. Using a spoon, scrape out most of the potato flesh, leaving a 1/4-inch-thick shell. (It's easier to scoop the potatoes when warm.) Cut the potato flesh into 1/2-inch dice and place in a bowl.

6. Add the bacon, 4 tablespoons of the butter, the scallions, and cheese to the potato flesh and gently stir to mix. Stir in the sour cream and salt and pepper to taste; the mixture should be highly seasoned. Stir as little and as gently as possible so as to leave some texture to the potatoes.

7. Spoon the potato mixture back into the potato shells, mounding it in the center. Top each potato half with a thin slice of the remaining butter and sprinkle with paprika. The potatoes can be prepared up to 24 hours ahead to this stage, covered, and refrigerated.

8. Just before serving, preheat your smoker to 400 °F. Add enough wood for 30 minutes of smoking. Place the potatoes in a shallow aluminum foil pan and re-smoke them until browned and bubbling, 15 to 20 minutes.

Smoked Mushrooms

Servings: 4

Cooking Time: 45 Minutes

Ingredients:

➢ Pound Mushrooms, fresh

➢ 1/2 Cup apple cider vinegar

➢ 1/2 Cup soy sauce

➢ 1 Teaspoon Blackened Saskatchewan Rub

Directions:

1. Clean mushrooms and place in a large Ziploc bag. Add apple cider vinegar, soy sauce and rub.

2. Mix well and allow to marinate in the refrigerator for at least 2 hours.

3. Supply your smoker with wood pellets and follow the start-up procedure. Preheat the grill, with the lid closed, to 350° F.

4. Place cast iron skillet inside grill for 20 minutes to warm up.

5. Add the mushrooms and marinade slowly into the cast iron skillet.

6. Cook uncovered for 15 minutes, then cover the skillet and cook another 30 minutes until mushrooms are tender. Grill: 350 °F

7. Remove skillet from grill and let mushrooms cool down for 5 minutes before serving. Enjoy!

Baked Breakfast Mini Quiches

Servings: 8

Cooking Time: 15 Minutes

Ingredients:

- ➢ cooking spray
- ➢ 1 Tablespoon extra-virgin olive oil
- ➢ 1/2 yellow onion, diced
- ➢ 3 Cup Spinach, fresh
- ➢ 10 eggs
- ➢ 4 Ounce shredded cheddar, mozzarella or Swiss cheese
- ➢ 1/4 Cup fresh basil
- ➢ 1 Teaspoon kosher salt
- ➢ 1/2 Teaspoon black pepper

Directions:

1. Spray a 12-cup muffin tin generously with cooking spray.

2. In a small skillet over medium heat, warm the oil. Add the onion and cook, stirring frequently, until softened, about 7 minutes. Add the spinach and cook until wilted, about 1 minute longer.

3. Transfer to a cutting board to cool, then chop the mixture so the spinach if broken up a little.

4. Supply your smoker with wood pellets and follow the start-up procedure. Preheat the grill, with the lid closed, to 350° F.

5. In a large bowl, whisk the eggs until frothy. Add the cooled onions and spinach, cheese, basil, 1 tsp salt and 1/2 tsp pepper. Stir to combine. Divide egg mixture evenly among the muffin cups.

6. Place tray on the grill and bake until the eggs have puffed up, are set, and are beginning to brown, about 18 to 20 minutes. Grill: 350 ˚F

7. Serve immediately, or allow to cool on a wire rack, then refrigerate in an air tight container for up to 4 days. Enjoy!

Smoked Bbq Onion Brussels Sprout

Servings: 4

Cooking Time: 110 Minutes

Ingredients:

➢ 4 strip bacon

➢ 1 onion minced

➢ 2 cloves garlic minced

➢ 1 lb brussels sprouts stems trimmed and cut in half

➢ 1 tbsp BBQ Spice Blend

➢ 1/2 cup Apple Habanero Bar-B-Que Sauce (or other BBQ sauce)

Directions:

1. Supply your smoker with wood pellets and follow the start-up procedure. Preheat the grill, with the lid closed, to High heat. Place a cast iron skillet over the highest heat spot and cook the bacon until crisp.

2. Remove the bacon from pan and drain, reserving the bacon fat in the pan.

3. Reduce the heat on your smoker to 250°F.

4. Add the onions, garlic, and brussels to the pan and toss to coat in the bacon drippings. Sprinkle the BBQ spice blend over top.

5. Cover the lid and allow to smoke for 1 to 1 1/2 hours, until the sprouts are fork tender.

6. For the last 20 minutes of smoking, toss the brussels sprouts in half of the barbecue sauce.

7. Remove the sprouts from the smoker.

8. Chop the bacon and add it and the remaining barbecue sauce to the pan of sprouts, tossing to coat.

9. Serve hot.

Spicy Asian Brussels Sprouts

Servings: 4

Cooking Time: 10 Minutes

Ingredients:

➤   2 Cup fresh Brussels sprouts

➤   2 Tablespoon vegetable oil

➤   1 Tablespoon Asian BBQ Rub

➤   1/4 Cup Thai sweet chile sauce

Directions:

1.   Supply your smoker with wood pellets and follow the start-up procedure. Preheat the grill, with the lid closed, to 350° F.

2.   Spread the halved brussel sprouts in a single layer on a lined cookie sheet. Drizzle with the oil and toss to coat.

3.   Sprinkle the brussel sprouts evenly with an Asian BBQ rub and put the cookie sheet on the grill. Close the lid and cook for 7-8 minutes. Grill: 350 ˚F

4.   Toss the brussels sprouts in the Thai Chili Sauce and return to the grill for an additional 3-4 minutes, or until the sprouts are crisp-tender. Grill: 350 ˚F

5.   Serve immediately. Enjoy!

Roasted Jalapeño Poppers

Servings: 2

Cooking Time: 30 Minutes

Ingredients:

- 8 Slices Bacon, Center Cut
- 2 Cup cream cheese
- 2 Ounce Cheese, sharp cheddar
- 1/2 Cup green onions, minced
- 2 Teaspoon fresh squeezed lime juice
- 4 Tablespoon Seeded Tomato, Chopped
- 4 Tablespoon cilantro, chopped
- 1/2 Teaspoon kosher salt
- 2 Small garlic clove, minced
- 12 Whole Jalapeños

Directions:

1. Supply your smoker with wood pellets and follow the start-up procedure. Preheat the grill, with the lid closed, to 350° F.

2. Place 2 bacon slices directly on the grill grate and cook 10-15 minutes until cooked through and crispy flipping halfway through. Remove from grill, but leave the grill on. When cool enough to handle, coarsely chop the bacon and reserve. Grill: 350 ˚F

3. In the bowl of a stand mixer, combine cream cheese, cheddar cheese, green onions, chopped bacon, lime juice, tomatoes, cilantro, salt and garlic. Mix on medium speed with a paddle until combined. Transfer mixture to a piping bag.

4. Cut the tops off the jalapeños and remove the seeds and ribs with a small paring knife.

5. Pipe the filling into each pepper so that the filling comes up a 1/4" over the top of the pepper. Place the tops back on each pepper.

6. With a rolling pin, flatten out the remaining six slices of bacon until they are 1/8" thick. Cut each slice in half. Wrap 1/2 a bacon slice around each pepper and secure with a toothpick.

7. Place the peppers in the Traeger Jalapeno Popper Tray. Place the tray directly on the grill grate and cook for 30-40 minutes until the peppers are tender, bacon is crispy, and cheese is melted. Enjoy! Grill: 350 ˚F

Baked Loaded Tater Tots

Servings: 6

Cooking Time: 35 Minutes

Ingredients:

- 2 Pound frozen tater tots
- 1 Can Black Beans
- 1 1/2 Cup leftover chili
- 1 Cup leftover queso
- 1 red onion, finely diced
- 1/2 Cup chopped cilantro
- 1/2 Cup sour cream
- 1 jalapeños, sliced

Directions:

1. Supply your smoker with wood pellets and follow the start-up procedure. Preheat the grill, with the lid closed, to 375° F.

2. Spread frozen tots out on a sheet tray and place directly on the grill grate.

3. Cook for 20 to 25 minutes or until tots are crispy. Grill: 375 ˚F

4. Top with warmed chili, queso and beans. Place back on the grill for 15 minutes. Grill: 375 ˚F

5. Remove from grill and top with red onion, cilantro, sour cream and jalapeño. Enjoy!

Smoked Pickled Green Beans

Servings: 4

Cooking Time: 45 Minutes

Ingredients:

- ➤ 1 Pound Green Beans, blanched
- ➤ 1/2 Cup salt
- ➤ 1/2 Cup sugar
- ➤ 1 Tablespoon red pepper flakes
- ➤ 2 Cup white wine vinegar
- ➤ 2 Cup ice water

Directions:

1. Supply your smoker with wood pellets and follow the start-up procedure. Preheat the grill, with the lid closed, to 180° F.

2. Place the blanched green beans on a mesh grill mat and place mat directly on the grill grate. Smoke the green beans for 30-45 minutes until they've picked up the desired amount of smoke. Remove from grill and set aside until the brine is ready. Grill: 180 °F

3. In a medium sized saucepan, bring all remaining ingredients, except ice water, to a boil over medium high heat on the stove. Simmer for 5-10 minutes then remove from heat and steep 20 minutes more. Pour brine over ice water to cool.

4. Once brine has cooled, pour over the green beans and weigh them down with a few plates to ensure they are completely submerged. Let sit 24 hours before use. Enjoy!

Mashed Red Potatoes

Servings: 4

Cooking Time: 40 Minutes

Ingredients:

- ➢ 8 Large red potatoes
- ➢ salt
- ➢ black pepper
- ➢ 1/2 Cup heavy cream
- ➢ 1/4 Cup butter

Directions:

1. Supply your smoker with wood pellets and follow the start-up procedure. Preheat the grill, with the lid closed, to 180° F.

2. Slice red potatoes in half, lengthwise then cut in half again to make quarters. Season potatoes with salt and pepper.

3. Increase the heat to High and preheat. Once the grill is hot, set potatoes directly on the grill grate. Grill: 450 °F

4. Every 15 minutes flip potatoes to ensure all sides get color. Continue to do this until potatoes are fork tender.

5. When tender, mash potatoes with cream, butter, salt, and pepper to taste. Serve warm, enjoy!

APPETIZERS AND SNACKS

Smoked Cashews

Servings: 6

Cooking Time: 60 Minutes

Ingredients:

➢   1 pound roasted, salted cashews

Directions:

1. Supply your smoker with wood pellets and follow the start-up procedure. Preheat the grill, with the lid closed, to 120°F.

2. Pour the cashews onto a rimmed baking sheet and smoke for 1 hour, stirring once about halfway through the smoking time.

3. Remove the cashews from the grill, let cool, and store in an airtight container for as long as you can resist.

Pigs In A Blanket

Servings: 4-6

Cooking Time: 15 Minutes

Ingredients:

- 2 Tablespoon Poppy Seeds
- 1 Tablespoon Dried Minced Onion
- 2 Teaspoon garlic, minced
- 2 Tablespoon Sesame Seeds
- 1 Teaspoon salt
- 8 Ounce Original Crescent Dough
- 1/4 Cup Dijon mustard
- 1 Large egg, beaten

Directions:

1. When ready to cook, start your smoker at 350 degrees F, and preheat with lid closed, 10 to 15 minutes.

2. Mix together poppy seeds, dried minced onion, dried minced garlic, salt and sesame seeds. Set aside.

3. Cut each triangle of crescent roll dough into thirds lengthwise, making 3 small strips from each roll.

4. Brush the dough strips lightly with Dijon mustard. Put the mini hot dogs on 1 end of the dough and roll up.

5. Arrange them, seam side down, on a greased baking pan. Brush with egg wash and sprinkle with seasoning mixture.

6. Bake in smoker until golden brown, about 12 to 15 minutes.

7. Serve with mustard or dipping sauce of your choice. Enjoy!

Chorizo Queso Fundido

Servings: 4-6   Cooking Time: 20 Minutes

Ingredients:

- 1 poblano chile
- 1 cup chopped queso quesadilla or queso Oaxaca
- 1 cup shredded Monterey Jack cheese
- ¼ cup milk
- 1 tablespoon all-purpose flour
- 2 (4-ounce) links Mexican chorizo sausage, casings removed
- ⅓ cup beer
- 1 tablespoon unsalted butter
- 1 small red onion, chopped
- ½ cup whole kernel corn
- 2 serrano chiles or jalapeño peppers, stemmed, seeded, and coarsely chopped
- 1 tablespoon minced garlic
- 1 tablespoon freshly squeezed lime juice
- 1 teaspoon ground cumin
- 1 teaspoon salt
- 1 teaspoon freshly ground black pepper
- 1 tablespoon chopped fresh cilantro
- 1 tablespoon chopped scallions
- Tortilla chips, for serving

Directions:

1. Supply your smoker with wood pellets and follow the start-up procedure. Preheat, with the lid closed, to 350°F.

2. On the smoker or over medium-high heat on the stove top, place the poblano directly on the grate (or burner) to char for 1 to 2 minutes, turning as needed. Remove from heat and place in a closed-up lunch-size paper bag for 2 minutes to sweat and further loosen the skin.

3. Remove the skin and coarsely chop the poblano, removing the seeds; set aside.

4. In a bowl, combine the queso quesadilla, Monterey Jack, milk, and flour; set aside.

5. On the stove top, in a cast iron skillet over medium heat, cook and crumble the chorizo for about 2 minutes.

6. Transfer the cooked chorizo to a small, grill-safe pan and place over indirect heat on the smoker.

7. Place the cast iron skillet on the preheated grill grate. Pour in the beer and simmer for a few minutes, loosening and stirring in any remaining sausage bits from the pan.

8. Add the butter to the pan, then add the cheese mixture a little at a time, stirring constantly.

9. When the cheese is smooth, stir in the onion, corn, serrano chiles, garlic, lime juice, cuvmin, salt, and pepper. Stir in the reserved chopped charred poblano.

10. Close the lid and smoke for 15 to 20 minutes to infuse the queso with smoke flavor and further cook the vegetables.

11. When the cheese is bubbly, top with the chorizo mixture and garnish with the cilantro and scallions.

12. Serve the chorizo queso fundido hot with tortilla chips.

Sriracha & Maple Cashews

Servings: 10

Cooking Time: 60 Minutes

Ingredients:

- 2 tbsp unsalted butter
- 3 tbsp pure maple syrup
- 1 tbsp sriracha
- 1 tsp coarse salt (use only if nuts are unsalted)
- 2½ cups unsalted cashews

Directions:

1. Supply your smoker with wood pellets and follow the start-up procedure. Preheat the grill, with the lid closed, to 250° F.

2. In a small saucepan on the stovetop over low heat, melt the butter. Add the maple syrup, sriracha, and salt (if using). Stir until combined. Add the nuts and stir gently to coat thoroughly.

3. Spread the nuts in a single layer in an aluminum foil roasting pan coated with cooking spray. Place the pan on the grate and smoke the nuts until they're lightly toasted, about 1 hour, stirring once or twice.

4. Remove the pan from the grill and let the nuts cool for 15 minutes. They'll be sticky at first but will crisp up. Break them up with your fingers and store at room temperature in an airtight container, such as a lidded glass jar.

Smoked Turkey Sandwich

Servings: 1

Cooking Time: 15 Minutes

Ingredients:

- 2 slices sourdough bread
- 2 tablespoons butter, at room temperature
- 2 (1-ounce) slices Swiss cheese
- 4 ounces leftover Smoked Turkey
- 1 teaspoon garlic salt

Directions:

1. Supply your smoker with wood pellets and follow the start-up procedure. Preheat the grill, with the lid closed, to 375°F.

2. Coat one side of each bread slice with 1 tablespoon of butter and sprinkle the buttered sides with garlic salt.

3. Place 1 slice of cheese on each unbuttered side of the bread, and then put the turkey on the cheese.

4. Close the sandwich, buttered sides out, and place it directly on the grill grate. Cook for 5 minutes. Flip the sandwich and cook for 5 minutes more. Remove the sandwich from the grill, cut it in half, and serve.

Grilled Guacamole

Servings: 6

Cooking Time: 30 Minutes

Ingredients:

- 3 large avocados, halved and pitted
- 1 lime, halved
- ½ jalapeño, deseeded and deveined
- ½ small white or red onion, peeled
- 2 garlic cloves, peeled and skewered on a toothpick
- 1 tsp coarse salt, plus more
- 1½ tbsp reduced-fat mayo
- 2 tbsp chopped fresh cilantro
- 2 tbsp crumbled queso fresco (optional)
- tortilla chips

Directions:

1. Supply your smoker with wood pellets and follow the start-up procedure. Preheat the grill, with the lid closed, to 225° F.

2. Place the avocados, lime, jalapeño, and onion cut sides down on the grate. Use the toothpicks to balance the garlic cloves between the bars. Smoke for 30 minutes. (You want the vegetables to retain most of their rawness.)

3. Transfer everything to a cutting board. Remove the garlic cloves from the toothpick and roughly chop. Sprinkle with the salt and continue to mince the garlic until it begins to form a paste. Scrape the garlic and salt into a large bowl.

4. Scoop the avocado flesh from the peels into the bowl. Squeeze the juice of ½ lime over the avocado. Mash the avocados but leave them somewhat chunky. Finely dice the jalapeño. Dice 2 tablespoons of onion. (Reserve the remaining onion for another use.) Add the jalapeño, onion, mayo, and cilantro to the bowl. Stir gently to combine. Taste for seasoning, adding more salt, lime juice, and jalapeño as desired.

5. Transfer the guacamole to a serving bowl. Top with the queso fresco (if using). Serve with tortilla chips.

Bacon-wrapped Jalapeño Poppers

Servings: 12

Cooking Time: 30 Minutes

Ingredients:

- 8 ounces cream cheese, softened
- ½ cup shredded Cheddar cheese
- ¼ cup chopped scallions
- 1 teaspoon chipotle chile powder or regular chili powder
- 1 teaspoon garlic powder
- 1 teaspoon salt
- 18 large jalapeño peppers, stemmed, seeded, and halved lengthwise
- 1 pound bacon (precooked works well)

Directions:

1. Supply your smoker with wood pellets and follow the start-up procedure. Preheat, with the lid closed, to 350°F. Line a baking sheet with aluminum foil.

2. In a small bowl, combine the cream cheese, Cheddar cheese, scallions, chipotle powder, garlic powder, and salt.

3. Stuff the jalapeño halves with the cheese mixture.

4. Cut the bacon into pieces big enough to wrap around the stuffed pepper halves.

5. Wrap the bacon around the peppers and place on the prepared baking sheet.

6. Put the baking sheet on the grill grate, close the lid, and smoke the peppers for 30 minutes, or until the cheese is melted and the bacon is cooked through and crisp.

7. Let the jalapeño poppers cool for 3 to 5 minutes. Serve warm.

Roasted Red Pepper Dip

Servings: 8   Cooking Time: 45 Minutes

Ingredients:

- 4 red bell peppers, halved, destemmed, and deseeded
- 1 cup English walnuts, divided
- 1 small white onion, peeled and coarsely chopped
- 2 garlic cloves, peeled and smashed with a chef's knife
- ¼ cup extra virgin olive oil, plus more
- 1 tbsp balsamic vinegar or balsamic glaze
- 1 tsp honey (eliminate if using balsamic glaze)
- 1 tsp coarse salt, plus more
- 1 tsp ground cumin
- 1 tsp smoked paprika
- ½ to 1 tsp Aleppo red pepper flakes, plus more
- ¼ cup fresh white breadcrumbs (optional)
- distilled water (optional)
- assorted crudités or wedges of pita bread

Directions:

1. Supply your smoker with wood pellets and follow the start-up procedure. Preheat the grill, with the lid closed, to 400° F.

2. Place the peppers skin side down on the grate and grill until the skins blister and the flesh softens, about 30 minutes. Transfer the peppers to a bowl and cover with plastic wrap. Let cool to room temperature. Remove the skins with a paring knife or your fingers. Coarsely chop or tear the peppers.

3. Place ¾ cup of walnuts in an aluminum foil roasting pan. Place the pan on the grate and toast for 10 to 15 minutes, stirring twice. Remove the pan from the grill and let the walnuts cool.

4. Place the peppers, onion, garlic, and walnuts in a food processor fitted with the chopping blade. Pulse several times. Add the olive oil, balsamic vinegar, honey, salt, cumin, paprika, and red pepper flakes. Process until the mixture is fairly smooth. Taste for seasoning, adding more salt or red pepper flakes (if desired). (If the mixture is too loose, add breadcrumbs until the texture is to your liking. If it's too thick, add olive oil or water 1 tablespoon at a time.)

5. Transfer the dip to a serving bowl. Use the back of a spoon to make a shallow depression in the center. Top with the remaining ¼ cup of walnuts and drizzle olive oil in the depression. Serve with crudités or pita bread.

Citrus-infused Marinated Olives

Servings: 6

Cooking Time: 30 Minutes

Ingredients:

- 1½ cups mixed brined olives, with pits
- ½ cup extra virgin olive oil
- 1 tbsp freshly squeezed lemon juice
- 1 garlic clove, peeled and thinly sliced
- 1 tsp smoked Spanish paprika
- 2 sprigs of fresh rosemary
- 2 sprigs of fresh thyme
- 2 bay leaves, fresh or dried
- 1 small dried red chili pepper, deseeded and flesh crumbled, or ¼ tsp crushed red pepper flakes
- 3 strips of orange zest
- 3 strips of lemon zest

Directions:

1. Supply your smoker with wood pellets and follow the start-up procedure. Preheat the grill, with the lid closed, to 180° F.

2. Drain the olives, reserving 1 tablespoon of brine. Spread the olives in a single layer in an aluminum foil roasting pan. Place the pan on the grate and cook the olives for 30 minutes, stirring the olives or shaking the pan once or twice.

3. In a small saucepan on the stovetop over low heat, warm the olive oil. Whisk in the lemon juice and the reserved 1 tablespoon of brine. Stir in the garlic and paprika. Add the rosemary, thyme, bay leaves, chili pepper, and orange and lemon zests. Warm over low heat for 10 minutes. Remove the saucepan from the heat.

4. Transfer the olives and olive oil mixture to a pint jar. Tuck the aromatics around the sides of the jar. Let cool and then cover and refrigerate for up to 5 days. Let the olives come to room temperature before serving.

Bayou Wings With Cajun Rémoulade

Servings: 8

Cooking Time: 40 Minutes

Ingredients:

- 16 large whole chicken wings or 32 drumettes and flats, about 3lb (1.4kg) total
- for the rub
- 1 tbsp kosher salt
- 1 tsp freshly ground black pepper
- 1 tsp paprika
- ½ tsp ground cayenne, plus more
- ½ tsp garlic powder
- ½ tsp celery salt
- ½ tsp dried thyme
- 2 tbsp vegetable oil
- for the rémoulade
- 1¼ cups reduced-fat mayo
- ¼ cup Creole-style or whole grain mustard
- 2 tbsp horseradish
- 2 tbsp pickle relish
- 1 tbsp freshly squeezed lemon juice
- 1 tsp paprika, plus more
- 1 tsp hot sauce, plus more
- 1 tsp Worcestershire sauce
- coarse salt
- for serving
- lemon wedges
- pickled okra (optional)

Directions:

1. Supply your smoker with wood pellets and follow the start-up procedure. Preheat the grill, with the lid closed, to 350° F.

2. If using whole wings, cut through the two joints, separating them into drumettes, flats, and wing tips. (Discard the wing tips or save them for chicken stock.) Alternatively, leave the wings whole. Place the chicken in a resealable plastic bag.

3. In a small bowl, make the rub by combining the ingredients. Mix well. Pour the rub over the wings and toss them to thoroughly coat. Refrigerate for 2 hours.

4. In a small bowl, make the Cajun rémoulade by whisking together the mayo, mustard, horseradish, pickle relish, lemon juice, paprika, hot sauce, and Worcestershire. Season with salt to taste. The mixture should be highly seasoned. Transfer to a serving bowl and lightly dust with paprika. Cover and refrigerate until ready to serve.

5. Remove the wings from the refrigerator and allow the excess marinade to drip off. Place the wings on the grate at an angle to the bars. Grill for 20 minutes and then turn. (They'll brown more evenly but will also have less of a tendency to stick.) Continue to cook until the wings are nicely browned and the meat is no longer pink at the bone, about 20 minutes more.

6. Remove the wings from the grill and pile them on a platter. Serve with the Cajun rémoulade, lemon wedges, and pickled okra (if using).

Deviled Eggs With Smoked Paprika

Servings: 6   Cooking Time: 30 Minutes

Ingredients:

- 6 large eggs
- 3 tbsp reduced-fat mayo, plus more
- 1 tsp Dijon or yellow mustard
- ½ tsp Spanish smoked paprika or regular paprika, plus more
- dash of hot sauce
- coarse salt
- freshly ground black pepper
- for garnishing
- small sprigs of fresh parsley, dill, tarragon, or cilantro
- chopped chives
- minced scallions
- Mustard Caviar
- sliced green or black olives
- celery leaves
- sliced radishes
- diced bell peppers
- sliced cherry tomatoes
- fresh or pickled jalapeños
- sliced or diced pickles
- slivers of sun-dried tomatoes
- bacon crumbles
- smoked salmon
- Hawaiian black salt
- Caviar

Directions:

1. Supply your smoker with wood pellets and follow the start-up procedure. Preheat the grill, with the lid closed, to 180° F.

2. On the stovetop over medium-high heat, bring a saucepan of water to a boil. (Make sure there's enough water in the saucepan to cover the eggs by 1 inch [5cm].) Use a slotted spoon to gently lower the eggs into the water. Lower the heat to maintain a simmer. Set a timer for 13 minutes.

3. Prepare an ice bath by combining ice and cold water in a large bowl. Carefully transfer the eggs to the ice bath when the timer goes off.

4. When the eggs are cool enough to handle, gently tap them all over to crack the shell. Carefully peel the eggs. Rinse under cold running water to remove any clinging bits of shell, but don't dry the eggs. (A damp surface will help the smoke adhere to the egg whites.)

5. Place the eggs on the grate and smoke until the eggs take on a light brown patina from the smoke, about 25 minutes. Transfer the eggs to a cutting board, handling them as little as possible.

6. Slice each egg in half lengthwise with a sharp knife. Wipe any yolk off the blade before slicing the next egg. Gently remove the yolks and place them in a food processor. Pulse to break up the yolks. Add the mayo, mustard, paprika, and hot sauce. Season with salt and pepper to taste. Pulse until the filling is smooth. Add additional mayo 1 teaspoon at a time if the mixture is a little dry. (It shouldn't be too loose either.)

7. Spoon the filling into each egg half or pipe it in using a small resealable plastic bag. You can also use a pastry bag fitted with a fluted tip.

8. Place the eggs on a platter and lightly dust with paprika. Accompany with one or more of the suggested garnishes.

Delicious Deviled Crab Appetizer

Servings: 30   Cooking Time: 10 Minutes

Ingredients:

- Nonstick cooking spray, oil, or butter, for greasing
- 1 cup panko breadcrumbs, divided
- 1 cup canned corn, drained
- ½ cup chopped scallions, divided
- ½ red bell pepper, finely chopped
- 16 ounces jumbo lump crabmeat
- ¾ cup mayonnaise, divided
- 1 egg, beaten
- 1 teaspoon salt
- 1 teaspoon freshly ground black pepper
- 2 teaspoons cayenne pepper, divided
- Juice of 1 lemon

Directions:

1. Supply your smoker with wood pellets and follow the start-up procedure. Preheat, with the lid closed, to 425°F.

2. Spray three 12-cup mini muffin pans with cooking spray and divide ½ cup of the panko between 30 of the muffin cups, pressing into the bottoms and up the sides. (Work in batches, if necessary, depending on the number of pans you have.)

3. In a medium bowl, combine the corn, ¼ cup of scallions, the bell pepper, crabmeat, half of the mayonnaise, the egg, salt, pepper, and 1 teaspoon of cayenne pepper.

4. Gently fold in the remaining ½ cup of breadcrumbs and divide the mixture between the prepared mini muffin cups.

5. Place the pans on the grill grate, close the lid, and smoke for 10 minutes, or until golden brown.

6. In a small bowl, combine the lemon juice and the remaining mayonnaise, scallions, and cayenne pepper to make a sauce.

7. Brush the tops of the mini crab cakes with the sauce and serve hot.

Pig Pops (sweet-hot Bacon On A Stick)

Servings: 24

Cooking Time: 30 Minutes

Ingredients:

- ➢ Nonstick cooking spray, oil, or butter, for greasing
- ➢ 2 pounds thick-cut bacon (24 slices)
- ➢ 24 metal skewers
- ➢ 1 cup packed light brown sugar
- ➢ 2 to 3 teaspoons cayenne pepper
- ➢ ½ cup maple syrup, divided

Directions:

1. Supply your smoker with wood pellets and follow the start-up procedure. Preheat, with the lid closed, to 350°F.
2. Coat a disposable aluminum foil baking sheet with cooking spray, oil, or butter.
3. Thread each bacon slice onto a metal skewer and place on the prepared baking sheet.
4. In a medium bowl, stir together the brown sugar and cayenne.
5. Baste the top sides of the bacon with ¼ cup of maple syrup.
6. Sprinkle half of the brown sugar mixture over the bacon.
7. Place the baking sheet on the grill, close the lid, and smoke for 15 to 30 minutes.
8. Using tongs, flip the bacon skewers. Baste with the remaining ¼ cup of maple syrup and top with the remaining brown sugar mixture.
9. Continue smoking with the lid closed for 10 to 15 minutes, or until crispy. You can eyeball the bacon and smoke to your desired doneness, but the actual ideal internal temperature for bacon is 155°F
10. Using tongs, carefully remove the bacon skewers from the grill. Let cool completely before handling.

Pulled Pork Loaded Nachos

Servings: 4   Cooking Time: 10 Minutes

Ingredients:

- 2 cups leftover smoked pulled pork
- 1 small sweet onion, diced
- 1 medium tomato, diced
- 1 jalapeño pepper, seeded and diced
- 1 garlic clove, minced
- 1 teaspoon salt
- 1 teaspoon freshly ground black pepper
- 1 bag tortilla chips
- 1 cup shredded Cheddar cheese
- ½ cup The Ultimate BBQ Sauce, divided
- ½ cup shredded jalapeño Monterey Jack cheese
- Juice of ½ lime
- 1 avocado, halved, pitted, and sliced
- 2 tablespoons sour cream
- 1 tablespoon chopped fresh cilantro

Directions:

1. Supply your smoker with wood pellets and follow the start-up procedure. Preheat, with the lid closed, to 375°F.

2. Heat the pulled pork in the microwave.

3. In a medium bowl, combine the onion, tomato, jalapeño, garlic, salt, and pepper, and set aside.

4. Arrange half of the tortilla chips in a large cast iron skillet. Spread half of the warmed pork on top and cover with the Cheddar cheese. Top with half of the onion-jalapeño mixture, then drizzle with ¼ cup of barbecue sauce.

5. Layer on the remaining tortilla chips, then the remaining pork and the Monterey Jack cheese. Top with the remaining onion-jalapeño mixture and drizzle with the remaining ¼ cup of barbecue sauce.

6. Place the skillet on the grill, close the lid, and smoke for about 10 minutes, or until the cheese is melted and bubbly. (Watch to make sure your chips don't burn!)

7. Squeeze the lime juice over the nachos, top with the avocado slices and sour cream, and garnish with the cilantro before serving hot.

POULTRY RECIPES

Chicken Tenders

Servings: 2-4

Cooking Time: 80 Minutes

Ingredients:

- ➢ 1 pound boneless, skinless chicken breast tenders
- ➢ 1 batch Chicken Rub

Directions:

1. Supply your smoker with wood pellets and follow the start-up procedure. Preheat the grill, with the lid closed, to 180°F.

2. Season the chicken tenders with the rub. Using your hands, work the rub into the meat.

3. Place the tenders directly on the grill grate and smoke for 1 hour.

4. Increase the grill's temperature to 300°F and continue to cook until the tenders' internal temperature reaches 170°F. Remove the tenders from the grill and serve immediately.

Chicken Parmesan Sliders With Pesto Mayonnaise

Servings: 4

Cooking Time: 30 Minutes

Ingredients:

- 2 Pound Chicken, ground
- 1 Cup Parmesan cheese
- 1 Tablespoon Worcestershire sauce
- black pepper
- 1 Cup mayonnaise
- 2 Tablespoon Pesto Sauce
- 3 Roma tomatoes
- 1 red onion, sliced
- Baby Spinach

Directions:

1. Line a baking sheet with plastic wrap. In a large mixing bowl, combine the ground chicken, the Parmesan, the Worcestershire, and a few grinds of black pepper. Wet your hands with cold water, and use them to mix the ingredients.

2. Divide the meat mixture in half, then form six 2-inch patties out of each half. Place the patties on the baking sheet, cover with another sheet of plastic wrap, and refrigerate for at least 1 hour.

3. Combine the mayonnaise and pesto in a small bowl and whisk together. Cover and refrigerate until serving time.

4. Supply your smoker with wood pellets and follow the start-up procedure. Preheat the grill, with the lid closed, to 300° F.

5. Arrange the chicken patties on the grill grate and grill, turning once, until the patties are cooked through (165F), about 30 minutes. Grill: 300 °F Probe: 165 °F

6. To serve, put a chicken patty on the bottom of a slider bun and top with a dollop of the pesto mayonnaise. Add tomato, onion, and spinach as desired. Replace the top of the bun and skewer with a frilled toothpick, if desired.

Smoked Drumsticks

Servings: 2-4

Cooking Time: 25 Minutes

Ingredients:

➢ 1 pound chicken drumsticks

➢ 2 tablespoons olive oil

➢ 1 batch Sweet and Spicy Cinnamon Rub

Directions:

1. Supply your smoker with wood pellets and follow the start-up procedure. Preheat the grill, with the lid closed, to 350°F.

2. Coat the drumsticks all over with olive oil and season with the rub. Using your hands, work the rub into the meat.

3. Place the drumsticks directly on the grill grate and smoke until their internal temperature reaches 170°F. Remove the drumsticks from the grill and serve immediately.

Savory Grilled Chicken Burrito Bowls

Servings: 4   Cooking Time: 20 Minutes

Ingredients:

- 1 Avocado
- 1 Can Black Beans, Rinsed And Drained
- 1 ½ Pounds Boneless Skinless Chicken Strips
- 1 Tablespoon Cilantro, Chopped
- 1 Can Corn Kernels, Drained
- Juice From 1 Lime
- ½ Lime Lime Juice

- 1 ½ Cups Long Grain White Rice
- 2 Tablespoons Olive Oil
- 2 Tablespoons Sweet Heat Rub
- ¼ Cup Salsa
- 1 Teaspoon Salt
- ½ Cup Shredded Mexican Blend Cheese
- ¼ Cup Sour Cream

Directions:

1. Supply your smoker with wood pellets and follow the start-up procedure. Preheat the grill, with the lid open, to 350° F. If using a gas or charcoal grill, set it up for medium heat.

2. Place the rice in a fine mesh sieve and rinse under cold water for 2-5 minutes, or until the water runs clear. Add the rice to a pot with 2 cups of water and 1 teaspoon of salt and bring to a boil on the stove top. Once the rice boils, drop the temperature to a simmer, place the pot lid on top securely, and let the rice cook for 20-25 minutes.

3. Once the time is up, remove the rice from the heat, and allow it to steam with the lid on for a further 10 minutes. Remove the lid from the rice, add the lime juice and cilantro, and fluff the rice with a fork. Set aside.

4. Grill the chicken for 5-7 minutes, or until the chicken reaches an internal temperature of 165°F and is golden and charred in some spots. Remove the chicken from the grill and allow it to rest for 5 minutes before slicing into bite sized pieces.

5. To assemble the burrito bowls: place a large scoop of cilantro lime rice into a bowl. Top with slices of grilled chicken, a scoop of black beans, a scoop of corn, salsa, cheese, sour cream, and avocado. Serve immediately.

Duck Breast With Pomegranate Sauce

Servings: 4   Cooking Time: 13 Minutes

Ingredients:

- 4 duck breasts, each about 6oz (170g), skin on
- for the rub
- 2 tsp coarse salt
- 1 tsp ground cumin
- 1 tsp ground coriander
- 1 tsp freshly ground black pepper
- ½ tsp ground cinnamon
- ½ tsp ground fennel
- for the sauce
- 1 shallot, peeled and minced
- 1 cup pomegranate juice
- 1 tbsp sherry vinegar or balsamic vinegar
- 1 tsp cornstarch
- ¼ cup chicken stock or chicken broth
- 1 tbsp chilled unsalted butter, cut into 4 pieces
- ¼ cup fresh pomegranate seeds (optional)
- 1 tbsp minced fresh chives

Directions:

1. Place a cast iron skillet on the grate. Supply your smoker with wood pellets and follow the start-up procedure. Preheat the grill, with the lid closed, to 400° F.

2. In a small bowl, make the rub by combining the ingredients. Use a sharp knife to diagonally score the skin of each duck breast—but don't nick the flesh. Lightly season the scored side of each breast.

3. Place the duck breasts skin side down in the skillet and sear until the skin is crisp and golden brown, about 8 to 10 minutes. Turn the breasts and cook until the internal temperature in the thickest part of a breast reaches 130°F (54°C), about 2 to 3 minutes more. Transfer the breasts to a plate.

4. In a large saucepan on the stovetop over medium heat, make the sauce by heating 1 tablespoon of duck fat from the skillet. (Reserve the remainder for another use.) Add the shallot and sauté until soft, about 2 to 3 minutes.

5. Add the pomegranate juice and bring the mixture to a boil over medium-high heat. Reduce the sauce by half, about 3 to 5 minutes. Add the vinegar and lower the heat to medium low.

6. Whisk together the cornstarch and chicken stock until smooth. Whisk into the sauce and cook until the sauce thickens, about 1 to 2 minutes. Whisk in the butter and stir in the pomegranate seeds (if using).

7. Place the duck breasts on a warm platter. Drizzle the pomegranate sauce over the top. Scatter the chives around the platter before serving.

Bbq Pulled Turkey Sandwiches

Servings: 6

Cooking Time: 120 Minutes

Ingredients:

- 6 Whole Turkey Thighs
- Pork & Poultry Rub
- 1 1/2 Cup chicken broth
- 1 Cup 'Que BBQ Sauce
- 6 Whole Kaiser Buns, Split

Directions:

1. Season turkey thighs on both sides with the Traeger Pork & Poultry rub.

2. Supply your smoker with wood pellets and follow the start-up procedure. Preheat the grill, with the lid closed, to 180° F.

3. Arrange the turkey thighs directly on the grill grate and smoke for 30 minutes.

4. Transfer the thighs to a sturdy disposable aluminum foil or roasting pan. Pour the broth around the thighs. Cover the pan with foil or a lid.

5. Increase temperature to 325°F and preheat, lid closed. Roast the thighs until they reach an internal temperature of 180°F. Grill: 325 °F Probe: 180 °F

6. Remove pan from the grill, but leave grill on. Let the turkey thighs cool slightly until they can be comfortably handled.

7. Pour off the drippings and reserve. Remove the skin and discard.

8. Pull the turkey meat into shreds with your fingers and return the meat to the roasting pan.

9. Add 1 cup or more of your favorite Traeger BBQ Sauce along with some of the drippings.

10. Recover the pan with foil and reheat the BBQ turkey on the Traeger for 20 to 30 minutes.

11. Serve with toasted buns if desired. Enjoy!

Smoked Maple Syrup Thanksgiving Turkey

Servings: 8

Cooking Time: 375 Minutes

Ingredients:

- 1 Cup Butter, Room Temp
- 1/2 Cup Maple Syrup
- 2 Tablespoons Champion Chicken Seasoning
- 1, (Pre-Brined) Turkey, Whole

Directions:

1. Supply your smoker with wood pellets and follow the start-up procedure. Preheat the grill, with the lid closed, to 250° F.

2. Combine the melted butter and maple syrup in a bowl. With the Marinade Injector, fill with the butter and syrup mixture and pierce the meat with the needle while pushing on the plunger, injecting the flavor. You want to inject the marinade into the thickest part of the breast, thigh, and wings.

3. Next, combine the room temperature butter and Champion Chicken seasoning and spread all over the turkey, making sure that you get it under the skin as well.

4. Place the turkey in an aluminum pan to catch all the drippings (this makes incredible gravy) and place on the grill.

5. When the breast and thigh meat of the turkey reaches 165°F to 170°F, remove from grill and let rest 15 minutes before carving. Happy Thanksgiving!

Smoked Turkey Wings

Servings: 2

Cooking Time: 60 Minutes

Ingredients:

➢ 4 turkey wings

➢ 1 batch Sweet and Spicy Cinnamon Rub

Directions:

1. Supply your smoker with wood pellets and follow the start-up procedure. Preheat the grill, with the lid closed, to 180°F.

2. Using your hands, work the rub into the turkey wings, coating them completely.

3. Place the wings directly on the grill grate and cook for 30 minutes.

4. Increase the grill's temperature to 325°F and continue to cook until the turkey's internal temperature reaches 170°F. Remove the wings from the grill and serve immediately.

Smoked Ditch Chicken

Servings: 2

Cooking Time: 60 Minutes

Ingredients:

➢ 3 pheasant breasts or quarters

➢ Blackened Saskatchewan Rub

➢ 3 Tablespoon Smoky Okie's Rooster Booster Poultry Seasoning

➢ 1 white onion

➢ 1 red bell pepper

➢ 4 Tablespoon olive oil

➢ salt and pepper

➢ 1 Box Uncle Ben's Ready Rice Pilaf

Directions:

1. Supply your smoker with wood pellets and follow the start-up procedure. Preheat the grill, with the lid closed, to 275° F.

2. Clean and rinse pheasant breasts and thighs; place in a large resealable bag.

3. Add a liberal amount of Traeger Blackened Saskatchewan Rub and Rooster Booster. Shake vigorously and set aside.

4. Slice the onions into thin sections. Quarter the peppers, removing the core.

5. Brush onions and peppers lightly with olive oil and lightly apply salt and pepper.

6. Place the vegetables on tin foil on one side of the grill. Give the vegetables an ample head start on the pheasant (at least an hour), as pheasant is lean and will cook quickly.

7. After allowing the vegetables to smoke for at least an hour, place the pheasant on the grill, keeping the grill at 275°F. Cook for 30 to 45 minutes. Remove the pheasant and vegetables from the grill and serve over a bed of rice pilaf. Enjoy! Grill: 275 °F

Bbq Game Day Chicken Wings And Thighs

Servings: 6

Cooking Time: 50 Minutes

Ingredients:

- ➢ 10 chicken thighs
- ➢ 30 chicken wings
- ➢ 1/2 Cup olive oil
- ➢ 1/2 Cup Chicken Rub

Directions:

1. Place thighs and wings in a large bowl. Add the olive oil and Traeger Chicken Rub and mix well. Cover bowl and refrigerate for 3 to 8 hours.

2. Supply your smoker with wood pellets and follow the start-up procedure. Preheat the grill, with the lid closed, to 375° F.

3. Place chicken directly on the grill grate and cook for 45 minutes. Check the internal temperature of the chicken, it is considered done at 165°F , however, a finished temperature of 175 to 180°F results in a better texture in dark meat. Grill: 375 °F Probe: 165 °F

4. Once the finished temperature is reached, remove chicken from the grill and let rest for 5 to 10 minutes before serving. Enjoy!

Texas Style Black Pepper Turkey

Servings: 6

Cooking Time: 240 Minutes

Ingredients:

- ➢ 1/2 Cup Coarse Black Pepper
- ➢ 1Lb Butter
- ➢ 1/2 Cup Salt, Kosher
- ➢ 1 Brined Turkey

Directions:

1. Supply your smoker with wood pellets and follow the start-up procedure. Preheat the grill, with the lid closed, to 300° F.

2. Liberally season Turkey with equal parts kosher salt and coarse black pepper.

3. Cook on grill until Internal temp reaches approximately 145°F or the skin has darkened to your liking.

4. Place turkey in a roasting pan topped with a pound of chopped butter and cover.

5. Return to the grill until internal temp of the thigh and breast reaches 165°F

6. Let rest for 30 minutes, carve and serve.

Smoked Quarters

Servings: 2-4

Cooking Time: 120 Minutes

Ingredients:

➤ 4 chicken quarters

➤ 2 tablespoons olive oil

➤ 1 batch Chicken Rub

➤ 2 tablespoons butter

Directions:

1. Supply your smoker with wood pellets and follow the start-up procedure. Preheat the grill, with the lid closed, to 180°F.

2. Coat the chicken quarters all over with olive oil and season them with the rub. Using your hands, work the rub into the meat.

3. Place the quarters directly on the grill grate and smoke for 1½ hours.

4. Baste the quarters with the butter and increase the grill's temperature to 375°F. Continue to cook until the chicken's internal temperature reaches 170°F.

5. Remove the quarters from the grill and let them rest for 10 minutes before serving.

Smoked Wings

Servings: 6

Cooking Time: 50 Minutes

Ingredients:

- ➢ 24 chicken wings, flats and drumettes separated
- ➢ 12 Ounce Italian dressing
- ➢ 3 Ounce Chicken Rub
- ➢ 5 Ounce 'Que BBQ Sauce
- ➢ 3 Ounce chili sauce

Directions:

1. Wash all wings and place into resealable bag. Add Italian dressing to the resealable bag containing the wings. Place in refrigerator and allow to marinate for 6 to 12 hours.

2. Supply your smoker with wood pellets and follow the start-up procedure. Preheat the grill, with the lid closed, to 225° F.

3. Remove wings from marinade and shake off excess marinade. Season all sides of the wings with Traeger Chicken Rub and let sit for 15 minutes before putting wings on the Traeger.

4. In a small bowl, combine the BBQ and chili sauces. Set aside.

5. Cook wings to an internal temperature of 160°F. Remove the wings and toss in chili barbecue sauce. Grill: 225 °F Probe: 160 °F

6. Increase the grill temperature to 375°F and preheat. Once at temperature, place the wings on the Traeger and sear both sides until the internal temperature reaches 165°F. Grill: 375 °F Probe: 165 °F

7. Remove the wings from grill and let rest for 5 minutes. Serve with your favorite side wing dressing or sauce. Enjoy!

Cajun Brined Maple Smoked Turkey Breast

Servings: 4

Cooking Time: 180 Minutes

Ingredients:

- 1 Gallon water
- 3/4 Cup canning and pickling salt
- 3 Tablespoon minced garlic
- 3 Tablespoon dark brown sugar
- 2 Tablespoon Worcestershire sauce
- 2 Tablespoon Cajun seasoning
- 1 (5-6 lb) bone-in turkey breast
- 3 Tablespoon extra-virgin olive oil
- 2 Tablespoon Cajun seasoning

Directions:

1. In a large food safe container or bucket, combine all of the ingredients for the brine with 1 gallon water. Stir until the salt is dissolved.

2. Place the turkey breast in the brine and weigh it down to ensure it is fully submerged. Cover and brine in a refrigerator for 1 to 2 days.

3. Remove the turkey breast from the brine and pat dry. Drizzle with the olive oil using your hands to cover all areas of the bird. Season liberally with Cajun seasoning. Probe: 165 °F

4. Supply your smoker with wood pellets and follow the start-up procedure. Preheat the grill, with the lid closed, to 225° F.

5. Place the turkey breast directly on the grill grate, close the lid and cook for 3 hours. After 3 hours, increase the temperature to 425°F and continue to cook for another 30 minutes or until the internal temperature reads 165°F when a thermometer is inserted into the thickest part of the breast. Grill: 225 °F Probe: 165 °F

6. Remove the turkey breast from the grill and allow to rest for at least 15 minutes before slicing. Slice and serve. Enjoy!

COCKTAILS RECIPES

Grilled Frozen Strawberry Lemonade

Servings: 4

Cooking Time: 15 Minutes

Ingredients:

- 1 Pound fresh strawberries
- 1/2 Cup turbinado sugar
- 8 lemon, halved
- 1/4 Cup Cointreau
- 1/4 Cup simple syrup
- 2 Cup ice
- 1 Cup Titos Vodka

Directions:

1. Supply your smoker with wood pellets and follow the start-up procedure. Preheat the grill, with the lid closed, to High heat.

2. Dip the lemon halves in turbinado sugar and place directly on the grill grate. Toss the strawberries with remaining sugar and place next to the lemons.

3. Cook until grill marks develop on both, about 15 min for lemons and 10 min for strawberries.

4. Remove from heat and let cool.

5. Juice grilled lemons straining out any seeds or pulp. Pour into a blender pitcher.

6. Remove stems from grilled strawberries and place in blender pitcher with lemon juice. Add simple syrup, vodka, cointreau, and 2 cups of ice.

7. Puree until smooth and transfer to 4-6 glasses. Garnish with grilled strawberries and grilled lemon slices if desired. Enjoy!

Grilled Peach Smash Cocktail

Servings: 2

Cooking Time: 10 Minutes

Ingredients:

- 2 peach, sliced and grilled
- 10 fresh mint leaves
- 1 1/2 Ounce Smoked Simple Syrup
- 4 Ounce bourbon
- 2 mint sprig, for garnish

Directions:

1. Supply your smoker with wood pellets and follow the start-up procedure. Preheat the grill, with the lid closed, to 375° F.

2. Cut the peach into 6 slices and brush with Traeger Smoked Simple Syrup. Place directly on the grill grate and cook 10 to 12 minutes or until peaches soften and get grill marks. Grill: 375 °F

3. In a mixing glass, add 3 slices of grilled peaches, 5 mint leaves and Traeger Smoked Simple Syrup.

4. Muddle ingredients to release oils of the mint and juices from the grilled peaches. Add bourbon and crushed ice.

5. Shake and pour into a stemless wine glass. Top off with more crushed ice. Garnish with a grilled peach and mint sprig. Enjoy!

Smoked Raspberry Bubbler Cocktail

Servings: 2

Cooking Time: 45 Minutes

Ingredients:

- 2 Cup fresh raspberries
- Smoked Simple Syrup
- 8 Ounce sparkling wine

Directions:

1. Supply your smoker with wood pellets and follow the start-up procedure. Preheat the grill, with the lid closed, to 180° F.

2. Smoked Raspberry Syrup: Place 1 cup fresh raspberries on a grill mat and smoke for 30 minutes. Grill: 180 ˚F

3. After the raspberries have been smoked, set a few aside for garnish. Place the remainder into a shallow sheet pan with Traeger Smoked Simple Syrup. Place back on the grill grate and let smoke for 45 minutes. Remove from heat and allow to cool. Strain and refrigerate until ready to use. Grill: 180 ˚F

4. Place 1 ounce of the smoked raspberry syrup in the bottom of a champagne flute and top off with sparkling white wine or champagne.

5. Garnish with smoked raspberries. Enjoy!

Grilled Peach Mint Julep

Servings: 2

Cooking Time: 45 Minutes

Ingredients:

- ➢ 2 Whole peach
- ➢ 4 Ounce whiskey
- ➢ 2 Cup sugar
- ➢ 4 Tablespoon pink peppercorns
- ➢ 20 Whole fresh mint leaves, plus more for garnish
- ➢ 2 lime wedge, for garnish
- ➢ 4 Ounce bourbon

Directions:

1. For the Grilled Whiskey Peaches: cut peach into slices, then soak peach slices in whiskey in the refrigerator for 4 to 6 hours.

2. For the Pink Peppercorn Simple Syrup: In a shallow pan, combine sugar, 1 cup water and pink peppercorns.

3. Supply your smoker with wood pellets and follow the start-up procedure. Preheat the grill, with the lid closed, to 180° F.

4. Cook syrup down on the grill for 30 minutes, or until desired smoke flavor has been reached. Remove from the grill. Grill: 180 ℉

5. Increase Traeger temperature to 350℉ and preheat. Place the whiskey peach slices directly on the grill grate and cook 10 to 12 minutes or until peaches soften and get grill marks. Grill: 350 ℉

6. To make the Julep: Muddle 1/2 ounce Pink Peppercorn Simple Syrup with 10 fresh mint leaves and 4 slices of grilled whiskey peaches.

7. Add crushed ice over the rim of the glass. Pour bourbon over the crushed ice and stir. Garnish with 1 large sprig of mint and fresh lime. Enjoy!

Traeger Smoked Daiquiri

Servings: 2

Cooking Time: 25 Minutes

Ingredients:

- ➤ 2 limes, sliced
- ➤ 2 Tablespoon granulated sugar
- ➤ 3 Ounce Rum
- ➤ 1 Ounce Smoked Simple Syrup
- ➤ 1 1/2 Ounce lime juice

Directions:

1. Supply your smoker with wood pellets and follow the start-up procedure. Preheat the grill, with the lid closed, to 350° F.

2. Toss the lime slices with granulated sugar and place directly on the grill grate. Cook 20-25 minutes or until grill marks form. Remove from grill and cool. Grill: 350 ˚F

3. In a mixing glass add rum, Traeger Simple Syrup, and fresh lime juice. Add ice to the mixing glass and shake. Strain contents into a chilled glass.

4. Garnish with a grilled lime wheel. Enjoy!

Smoked Sangria

Servings: 6

Cooking Time: 45 Minutes

Ingredients:

- ➢ 1 (750 ml) medium-bodied red wine
- ➢ 1/4 Cup Grand Marnier
- ➢ 1/4 Cup Smoked Simple Syrup
- ➢ 1 Cup fresh cranberries
- ➢ 1 Whole apple, sliced
- ➢ 2 Whole limes, sliced
- ➢ 4 cinnamon stick
- ➢ soda water

Directions:

1.   Supply your smoker with wood pellets and follow the start-up procedure. Preheat the grill, with the lid closed, to 180° F.

2.   In a shallow dish, combine red wine, Grand Marnier, Traeger Smoked Simple Syrup and cranberries, and place directly on the grill grate.

3.   Smoke for 30 to 45 minutes or until the liquid picks up desired amount of smoke. Remove from grill and place in the fridge to cool. Grill: 180 ℉

4.   When the mixture has cooled, place in a large pitcher. Add sliced apples, limes, cinnamon sticks and ice to pitcher.

5.   Top with soda water, if desired. Enjoy!

Smoked Eggnog

Servings: 4

Cooking Time: 60 Minutes

Ingredients:

➢   2 Cup whole milk

➢   1 Cup heavy cream

➢   4 egg yolk

➢   Cup sugar

➢   3 Ounce bourbon

➢   1 Teaspoon vanilla extract

➢   1 Teaspoon nutmeg

➢   4 egg white

➢   whipped cream

Directions:

1.   Plan ahead, this recipe requires chill time.

2.   Supply your smoker with wood pellets and follow the start-up procedure. Preheat the grill, with the lid closed, to 180° F.

3.   Pour the milk and the cream into a baking pan and smoke on the Traeger for 60 minutes. Grill: 180 °F

4.   Meanwhile, in the bowl of a stand mixer, beat the egg yolks until they lighten in color. Gradually add 1/3 cup sugar and continue to beat until sugar completely dissolves.

5.   After the milk and cream have smoked, add them along with the bourbon, vanilla and nutmeg into the egg mixture and stir to combine.

6.   Place the egg whites in the bowl of a stand mixer and beat to soft peaks. When you lift the beaters the whites will make a peak that slightly curls down.

7.   With the mixer still running, gradually add 1 tablespoon of sugar and beat until stiff peaks form.

8.   Gently fold the egg whites into the cream mixture and then whisk to thoroughly combine.

9.   Chill eggnog for a couple hours to let the flavors meld. Garnish with a dash of nutmeg and whipped cream on top. Enjoy!

Smoked Barnburner Cocktail

Servings: 2

Cooking Time: 45 Minutes

Ingredients:

- ➢ 16 Ounce fresh raspberries
- ➢ 1/2 Cup Smoked Simple Syrup
- ➢ 1 1/2 Ounce smoked raspberry syrup
- ➢ 3 Ounce reposado tequila
- ➢ 1 Ounce lime juice
- ➢ 1 Ounce lemon juice
- ➢ 2 grilled lime wheel, for garnish

Directions:

1. Supply your smoker with wood pellets and follow the start-up procedure. Preheat the grill, with the lid closed, to 180° F.

2. For Smoked Raspberry Syrup: Place fresh raspberries on a grill mat and smoke for 30 minutes. After the raspberries have been smoked, reserve a few for garnish and place the remainder into a shallow sheet pan with Traeger Smoked Simple Syrup. Grill: 180 ℉

3. Place sheet pan on the grill grate and smoke for 45 minutes. Remove from grill and let cool. Strain through a fine mesh sieve discarding solids. Transfer the syrup to the refrigerator until ready to use. Makes about 1/2 cup of smoked raspberry syrup. Grill: 180 ℉

4. For cocktail: Add 3/4 ounce smoked raspberry syrup, tequila, lime juice and lemon juice with ice into a mixing glass. Shake and pour over clean ice. Garnish with smoked raspberries and a grilled lime wheel. Enjoy!

Honey Glazed Grapefruit Shandy Cocktail

Servings: 2

Cooking Time: 20 Minutes

Ingredients:

- 4 grapefruits
- 4 Tablespoon honey
- granulated sugar
- 2 Ounce bourbon
- 1 Ounce Smoked Simple Syrup
- 4 Ounce honey glazed grilled grapefruit, juiced
- 2 Bottle Ballast Point Grapefruit Sculpin

Directions:

1. Supply your smoker with wood pellets and follow the start-up procedure. Preheat the grill, with the lid closed, to 375° F.

2. For the honey glazed grapefruit: Slice one grapefruit in half and coat with 2 tablespoons honey.

3. Take the other grapefruit and slice into wheels. Toss the wheels in granulated sugar until well coated.

4. Place the grapefruit halves and wheels directly on the grill grate, cut side down, and cook for 20 to 30 minutes. Remove from grill and set the wheels aside. Grill: 375 °F

5. Squeeze the grapefruit halves into a measuring cup. It should yield about 2 oz juice.

6. Pour the grapefruit juice into a shaker and add bourbon and Traeger Smoked Simple Syrup then top with ice. Shake for 10-15 seconds.

7. Strain into glass, add ice and fill with beer. Garnish with the grilled grapefruit wheel. Enjoy!

Smoke And Bubz Cocktail

Servings: 2

Cooking Time: 45 Minutes

Ingredients:

➢ 16 Ounce POM Juice

➢ 2 Cup pomegranate seeds

➢ 6 Ounce sparkling white wine

➢ 2 lemon twist, for garnish

➢ 2 Teaspoon pomegranate seeds

Directions:

1. Supply your smoker with wood pellets and follow the start-up procedure. Preheat the grill, with the lid closed, to 180° F.

2. For the Smoked Pomegranate Juice: Pour POM juice and a cup of pomegranate seeds into a shallow sheet pan. Smoke on the Traeger for 45 minutes. Pull off grill, strain, discard seeds and let sit until chilled. Grill: 180 ℉

3. Add 1-1/2 ounces of the smoked pomegranate juice to the bottom of a champagne flute.

4. Add sparkling white wine, a few fresh pomegranate seeds and a lemon twist to garnish. Enjoy!

Smoky Mountain Bramble Cocktail

Servings: 2

Cooking Time: 15 Minutes

Ingredients:

- 16 Ounce blackberries
- 2 Cup sugar
- 10 smoked blackberries
- 3 Ounce vodka
- 1 1/2 Ounce Alpine Distilling Preserve Liqueur
- 1 1/2 Ounce lemon juice
- 1 Ounce smoked blackberry syrup

Directions:

1. Supply your smoker with wood pellets and follow the start-up procedure. Preheat the grill, with the lid closed, to 180° F.

2. To make Smoked Blackberry Simple Syrup: Place blackberries on a grill mat and smoke for 15 to 20 minutes. Grill: 180 °F

3. Combine 1 cup water and sugar in a small sauce pan and warm over medium heat until sugar dissolves. Remove from heat and place 2/3 of blackberries in the simple syrup and macerate.

4. Strain through a fine mesh strainer and store for up to 14 days.

5. To make the cocktail: Muddle 4 to 5 smoked blackberries in a cocktail shaker. Add vodka, Preserve Liqueur, lemon and smoked blackberry syrup. Add ice and shake vigorously. Double strain into an old fashioned glass.

6. Garnish with a smoked blackberry and lemon twist. Enjoy!

Dublin Delight Cocktail

Servings: 2

Cooking Time: 20 Minutes

Ingredients:

- ➢ 2 orange, sliced
- ➢ 3 Fluid Ounce Teeling Whiskey
- ➢ 1 1/2 Fluid Ounce Smoked Simple Syrup
- ➢ 6 Dash aromatic bitters
- ➢ 6 Fluid Ounce Guinness beer
- ➢ 2 Amarena cherry, for garnish

Directions:

1. Supply your smoker with wood pellets and follow the start-up procedure. Preheat the grill, with the lid closed, to 450° F.

2. Place orange slices directly on the grill grate and cook 20 to 25 minutes. Remove from grill and let cool. Grill: 450 °F

3. In a mixing glass, add whiskey, Traeger Smoked Simple Syrup and bitters. Add ice and shake. Pour over a beer glass filled with ice and top off with cold Guinness.

4. Garnish with a grilled orange slice and Amarena cherry. Enjoy!

Smoked Cold Brew Coffee

Servings: 8

Cooking Time: 120 Minutes

Ingredients:

- 12 Ounce coarse ground coffee
- heavy cream or milk
- sugar

Directions:

1. Place half the coffee grounds in a plastic container and slowly pour 3-1/2 cups water over the top of the grounds. Add remaining grounds and pour another 3-1/2 cups water over the top in a circular motion.

2. Press the grounds down into the water using the back of a spoon. Cover and transfer to the refrigerator and let sit for 18 to 24 hours.

3. Remove from refrigerator and strain into a clean container through a fine mesh strainer or double layer of cheese cloth.

4. Supply your smoker with wood pellets and follow the start-up procedure. Preheat the grill, with the lid closed, to 180° F.

5. Pour cold brew into a shallow baking dish and place directly on the grill grate. Smoke for 1 to 2 hours depending on desired level of smoke. Grill: 180 °F

6. Remove from grill and place over an ice bath to cool. Drink as is over ice, with cream or sugar or use in your favorite coffee recipes. Enjoy!

Smoked Hot Buttered Rum

Servings: 4

Cooking Time: 30 Minutes

Ingredients:

- 2 Cup water
- 1/4 Cup brown sugar
- 1/2 Stick butter, melted
- 1 Teaspoon ground cinnamon
- 1/4 Teaspoon ground nutmeg
- ground cloves
- salt
- 6 Ounce Rum

Directions:

1. Supply your smoker with wood pellets and follow the start-up procedure. Preheat the grill, with the lid closed, to 180° F.

2. In a shallow baking dish, combine 2 cups water with all ingredients except for the rum and place directly on the grill grate. Smoke for 30 minutes. Grill: 180 ℉

3. Remove from the grill and pour into the pitcher of a blender. Process until somewhat frothy.

4. Pour 1.5 ounces of rum each into 4 glasses. Split hot butter mixture evenly between the four glasses.

5. Garnish with a cinnamon stick and freshly grated nutmeg. Enjoy!

BEEF LAMB AND GAME RECIPES

Cheesy Nachos

Servings: 8   Cooking Time: 20 Minutes

Ingredients:

- Cilantro
- Olive Oil
- Pepper
- 1 Red Bell Peppers, Sliced
- 2 Rib-Eye Steaks
- Salsa
- Salt
- 1 Cup Shredded Cheddar Cheese
- Sour Cream
- 1 Yellow Bell Pepper, Sliced
- 1 Zucchini, Sliced

Directions:

1. Supply your smoker with wood pellets and follow the start-up procedure. Preheat the grill, with the lid closed, to 400° F.

2. Coat both sides of the steak with olive oil and season with sea salt and pepper. Place the steak on the grates and grill for about 4 to 5 minutes per side.

3. Remove the steak off the grill and let rest for about 10 minutes before cutting into bite-sized strips.

4. Brush with barbecue sauce if desired.

5. Empty a large bag of nacho chips evenly into a cast iron pan. Start loading up with toppings - steak, cheddar cheese, sautéed vegetables.

6. These are just suggested toppings, so feel free to add anything you like!

7. Place your loaded nachos on the grill and let the hot smoke melt your toppings into one hearty creation.

8. Cook for about 10 minutes, or until the cheese has fully melted.

9. Remove and serve with sour cream and salsa.

Zucchini Onion Meatloaf

Servings: 8   Cooking Time: 180 Minutes

Ingredients:

- 3 Pounds Ground Beef
- 1 Pound Italian Sausage
- 1/2 Cup Diced Onion
- 1/2 Cup Diced Green Pepper
- 1 Cup Shredded Fresh Zucchini
- 1 Egg
- 3/4 Cup Ketchup
- 1 Sleeve Crackers, Crushed (Buttery Or Saltine)
- 4 Slices Bread, Cubed
- 1/3 Cup Grated Parmesan Cheese
- 1/4 Teaspoon Each Salt and Pepper to Taste
- Garnish:
- Onion Slices, For Eyes
- 1 Pound Thick Sliced Bacon, for Bandages
- Green Pepper Slices, Nose and Teeth
- Sweet Ketchup Sauce:
- 2 Cups Ketchup
- 1/3 Cup Brown Sugar
- 1 Tablespoon Worcestershire Sauce
- 1/2 Teaspoon Onion Powder
- 1/2 Teaspoon Garlic Powder

Directions:

1. Supply your smoker with wood pellets and follow the start-up procedure. Preheat the grill, with the lid closed, to 350 °F.

2. In a large bowl mix together all ingredients.

3. Place mixture into a 13 x 9 inch baking dish and shape into a skull.

4. Place onion slices on meatloaf where the eyes should beand green pepper slices for teeth.

5. Randomly place bacon slices on meatloaf skull to look like bandages.

6. Bake meatloaf in your grill, covered with foil for 2 hours (drain excess grease if necessary).

7. Remove foil, and continue baking for another hour (drain excess grease if necessary).

8. Meanwhile, in a small saucepan, stir together ketchup, brown sugar, Worcestershire sauce, onion powder,and garlic powder. Put in the grill grate and simmer on low until warm. Baste meatloaf with sauce every 15 minutes during last hour of baking.

9. Serve with remaining sauce.

Flavour Smoked Chuck Roast

Servings: 6

Cooking Time: 540 Minutes

Ingredients:

- ➤ 3 cups beef stock, divided
- ➤ 1, 3 lb chuck roast
- ➤ 3 tbsp sweet heat rub
- ➤ 1 yellow onion

Directions:

1. Place chuck roast in a 9x13 baking pan. Sprinkle generously with Sweet Heat Rub and rub to coat evenly on all sides.

2. Cover pan with foil and refrigerate overnight.

3. The next day, remove chuck roast from refrigerator and let it come to room temperature.

4. Supply your smoker with wood pellets and follow the start-up procedure. Preheat the grill, with the lid closed, to 225° F. If using a gas or charcoal grill, set it for low heat.

5. Insert a temperature probe into the thickest side of the roast, then place chuck roast directly on grill grate. Close lid and smoke for 3 hours.

6. Spray roast with 1 cup of beef stock every hour.

7. Slice the onion and place in a 9x13 aluminum pan. Pour the remaining cup of stock over the onions and set roast on top of onions.

8. Increase temperature to 250°F and cook an additional 2 ½ to 3 hours, or until internal temperature reaches 165°F.

9. Once 165°F internal temperature is reached, cover roast with aluminum foil, and cook another 2 ½ to 3 hours, or until internal temperature reaches 200°F.

10. Remove chuck roast from grill.

11. Allow roast to rest 15 minutes, then remove from pan and shred with meat claws. For added moistness and flavor, pour some remaining cooking stock over the shredded roast and serve.

Reuben Sandwich

Servings: 4

Cooking Time: 10 Minutes

Ingredients:

- ➢ 2 Cup mayonnaise
- ➢ 1/2 Cup ketchup
- ➢ 1/4 Cup pickle relish
- ➢ 2 Tablespoon Chicken Rub
- ➢ 4 Pound leftover corned beef, thinly sliced
- ➢ 2 1/2 Cup sauerkraut
- ➢ 10 Slices Swiss cheese
- ➢ 10 Slices marble rye bread
- ➢ 6 Tablespoon butter, room temperature

Directions:

1. See Traeger Smoked Corned Beef Brisket recipe for corned beef instructions.

2. Supply your smoker with wood pellets and follow the start-up procedure. Preheat the grill, with the lid closed, to 350° F.

3. Place a large griddle directly on the grill grate to heat up while the sandwiches are being assembled.

4. Combine the mayonnaise, ketchup, relish and Traeger Chicken Rub in a bowl and stir until well mixed.

5. Butter the outsides of the bread (the side that goes on the grill). Place a layer of sauce on the other side of the bread and top with the corned beef, sauerkraut and 2 Swiss cheese slices. Top with another slice of sauced bread.

6. Place sandwiches on the hot griddle in the Traeger and cook for 5 minutes. Using a spatula, flip the sandwiches and cook for an additional 5 minutes, or until toasted with melty cheese and warm meat. Grill: 350 °F

7. Remove sandwiches from the Traeger. Enjoy!

Diva Q's Herb-crusted Prime Rib

Servings: 4

Cooking Time: 300 Minutes

Ingredients:

➢ 1/4 Cup fresh rosemary leaves

➢ 1/4 Cup fresh flat-leaf parsley leaves

➢ 1/4 Cup minced garlic

➢ 1/4 Cup canola oil

➢ 3 Tablespoon Dijon mustard

➢ 2 Tablespoon finely ground black pepper

➢ 2 Tablespoon kosher salt

➢ 1 (5-7 lb) bone-in prime rib roast

Directions:

1. Combine rosemary, parsley, garlic, canola oil, mustard, salt and pepper in a food processor. Pulse until the herbs are finely chopped and the ingredients are combined.

2. Coat the entire prime rib with the herb mixture. Refrigerate prime rib uncovered, for 4 hours.

3. Supply your smoker with wood pellets and follow the start-up procedure. Preheat the grill, with the lid closed, to 250° F.

4. Place the prime rib bone side down on the grill. Roast meat (allowing 12 to 15 minutes per pound) until the internal temperature in the thickest part of the prime rib reaches 120°F-130°F for rare to medium-rare, about 5 hours. Begin taking the internal temperature every 45 minutes after the 2 hour mark. Grill: 250 °F Probe: 120 °F

5. Remove the prime rib from the grill, tent loosely with foil and let rest for 15 minutes before slicing. Enjoy!

Green Chile Cheese Beef Sliders

Servings: 8 - 10

Cooking Time: 480 Minutes

Ingredients:

- ➤ Aluminum Foil Aluminum Foil
- ➤ 1 Can Beef Broth
- ➤ 1 Package Slider Buns
- ➤ Cheddar Cheese, Slices
- ➤ 1 5-6Lbs Trimmed Beef Chuck Roast
- ➤ 1 Can Green Chiles, Diced
- ➤ 7 Oz Jar Salsa Verde
- ➤ 2 Tablespoons Sweet Heat Rub

Directions:

1. Supply your smoker with wood pellets and follow the start-up procedure. Preheat the grill, with the lid closed, to 300° F. If you're using a gas or charcoal grill, set the temperature to medium heat.

2. Remove the beef chuck roast from its packaging, drain any excess fluid, and pat it dry with paper towels.

3. Place the chuck roast in a disposable aluminum pan. Pour the salsa verde, diced green chiles, Sweet Heat Rub, and beef broth over the top of the roast.

4. Place a temperature probe into the thickest part of the chuck roast and tightly wrap the top of the pan in aluminum foil to seal it.

5. Grill for 5-6 hours, or until the beef is at an internal temperature of 202°F and is tender and falling apart.

6. Remove the chuck roast from the grill and allow it to rest for 30 minutes.

7. Once the chuck roast has finished resting, use the Meat Claws to shred the beef, discarding any fatty parts.

8. Top the slider buns with a slice of Cheddar cheese and a spoonful of the Green Chile Shredded Beef, and serve immediately.

Smoked Moink Burger By Scott Thomas

Servings: 4

Cooking Time: 60 Minutes

Ingredients:

- 1 Pound Ground Sirloin
- 1/2 Pound ground pork
- 1/4 Cup Worcestershire sauce
- 1 Teaspoon garlic, minced
- salt
- black pepper

Directions:

1. Combine all the ingredients in a bowl and mix together. Form into six patties.

2. Supply your smoker with wood pellets and follow the start-up procedure. Preheat the grill, with the lid closed, to 350° F.

3. Cook until the burgers reach an internal temperature of 160 degrees F (about an hour depending on the size of the patties and the heat of the grill).

4. Top with your favorite cheese to melt a few minutes before burgers are done and serve with your favorite toppings.

Traditional Tomahawk Steak

Servings: 4-6

Cooking Time: 120 Minutes

Ingredients:

- ➢ 1 tomahawk ribeye steak (2 1/2 to 3 1/2 lbs)
- ➢ 5 garlic cloves, minced
- ➢ 2 tbsp kosher salt
- ➢ 1 bundle fresh thyme
- ➢ 2 tbsp ground black pepper
- ➢ 8 oz butter stick
- ➢ 1 tbsp garlic powder
- ➢ 1/8 cup olive oil

Directions:

1. Mix rub ingredients (salt, black pepper, and garlic powder) in a small bowl. Use this mixture to season all sides of the ribeye steak generously. You can also substitute your favorite steak seasoning. After applying seasoning, let the steak rest at room temperature for at least 30 minutes.

2. While the steak rests, preheat your pellet grill to 450°F - 550°F for searing

3. Sear the steak for 5 minutes on each side. Halfway through each side (so after 2 1/2 minutes), rotate the steak 90° to form grill marks on the tomahawk

4. After the tomahawk steak has seared for 5 minutes on each side (10 minutes total), move the steak to a raised rack

5. Adjust your pellet grill's temperature to 250°F and turn up smoke setting if applicable. Leave the lid open for a moment to help allow some heat to escape

6. Stick your probe meat thermometer into the very center of the cut to measure internal temperature.

7. Place butter stick, garlic cloves, olive oil, and thyme in the aluminum pan. Then place the aluminum pan under the steak to catch drippings. After a few minutes, the steak drippings and ingredients will mix together

8. Baste the steak with the aluminum pan mixture every 10 minutes until the tomahawk steak reaches your desired doneness

9. Once the steak reaches its desired doneness, remove from the grill and place on a cutting board or serving dish. The steak should rest for 10-15 minutes before cutting/serving.

Texas Hill Country Brisket With Mustard Barbecue Sauce

Servings: 10-12   Cooking Time: 660 Minutes

Ingredients:

- 1 whole packer brisket, about 12 to 14lb (5.4 to 6.4kg)
- for the sauce
- ½ cup yellow mustard
- ½ cup brown mustard
- ½ cup apple cider vinegar
- ¼ cup light brown sugar or low-carb substitute, plus more
- 1 tbsp ketchup
- 1 tbsp Worcestershire sauce
- 1 tbsp hot sauce
- 1 tsp beef bouillon granules
- 1 tsp granulated garlic
- 1 tsp coarse salt, plus more
- ½ tsp freshly ground black pepper
- for the rub
- ¼ cup coarse salt
- ¼ cup fresh coarsely ground black pepper
- 1 tbsp granulated garlic
- 1 tbsp chili powder

Directions:

1. Place a pan of water on the grate.Supply your smoker with wood pellets and follow the start-up procedure. Preheat the grill, with the lid closed, to 250° F.

2. In a medium saucepan on the stovetop over medium-low heat, make the sauce by whisking together the ingredients. Bring the mixture to a simmer, stirring occasionally. Simmer for 10 minutes. Taste, adding brown sugar or salt. Transfer the sauce to a covered jar and refrigerate until ready to use.

3. In a small bowl, make the rub by combining the ingredients. Trim some of the excess exterior fat off the brisket, leaving a cap of at least ¼ inch (.5cm). Place the brisket on a rimmed baking sheet. Evenly but conservatively season the meat on all sides with the rub.

4. Place the brisket fat side down on the grate and smoke until the internal temperature reaches 165°F (74°C), about 5 to 6 hours.

5. Remove the brisket from the grill and wrap it fat side up in unlined butcher paper, crimping the seams. (You can also use aluminum foil—many well-known Texas pitmasters do—but it's not as porous.) Return the brisket seam side up to the grate. Continue to cook until the internal temperature reaches 203°F (95°C), about 6 to 8 hours more. The meat should be very tender, with the melted collagen making it almost jiggly.

6. Transfer the brisket to an insulated cooler lined with clean towels or a thick layer of newspapers. Let the meat rest for 1 to 2 hours.

7. Place the brisket on a cutting board and unwrap it. Separate the point from the flat following the seam of fat that runs between them. Use a serrated knife to slice the meat against the grain into pencil-thick pieces. (The grain in the point runs perpendicular to the grain in the flat.)

8. Shingle the meat on a platter. Drizzle with any meat juices from the cutting board. Serve with the barbecue sauce.

Smoked Texas Bbq Brisket

Servings: 8

Cooking Time: 600 Minutes

Ingredients:

➢ 1 (14-18 lb) whole packer brisket
➢ Meat Church Holy Cow BBQ Rub
➢ Meat Church Holy Gospel BBQ Rub

Directions:

1. Trim any hard fat from all sides of the brisket, being careful not to dig too deep into the meat. Trim the sides of any excess or loose fat. Trim the fat side of the brisket to 1/4 inch thick.

2. Season all sides evenly with Meat Church Holy Cow Rub. Optionally add a light layer of Meat Church Holy Gospel Rub. Let the brisket sit in the seasoning at room temp for 20 to 30 minutes.

3. Supply your smoker with wood pellets and follow the start-up procedure. Preheat the grill, with the lid closed, to 275° F.

4. Place the brisket fat side up on the grill grate. Cook until it reaches an internal temperature of 165°F, about 5 to 6 hours

5. Remove brisket and wrap tightly in Traeger Butcher Paper.

6. Place the wrapped brisket back on the grill and cook until it reaches an internal temperature of 204°F, about 3-4 hours. Grill: 275 °F Probe: 204 °F

7. When the brisket reaches 204°F, remove from grill and let rest for 30 minutes. When ready to eat, unwrap brisket and slice against the grain. Enjoy!

Lemon Tomahawk Steak

Servings: 2 – 4

Cooking Time: 215 Minutes

Ingredients:

- Apple Corer Or Metal Spoon
- 3 Lbs Gala Apples
- 1 Lemon
- Chop House Steak Rub
- 1 Tbsp Tennessee Apple Butter Rub
- Sugar
- 4 Cups Water

Directions:

1. Supply your smoker with wood pellets and follow the start-up procedure. Preheat the grill, with the lid closed, to 400° F. If using a gas or charcoal grill, set heat to medium-high heat.

2. Core and halve the apples. Place apples skin-side down on a sheet tray and season with Tennessee Apple Butter and set aside.

3. In a cast iron pot, combine the apple cores with the juice and zest from one lemon. Cover the mixture with water, transfer to the grill and bring to a boil. Reduce heat to 225° F. Place the apples directly on the grill grate (skin-side down) and cook for 1 hour.

4. After 1 hour, remove cast iron pot from the grill. Strain liquid, discard cores, return liquid to pot, and whisk in sugar. Cover with lid and return to grill. Allow to simmer for another hour.

5. Add smoked apples to the pot and continue to simmer for 20 minutes. Remove pot from grill and purée apple mixture in a blender. Pour apple purée back into pot and return to grill. Increase heat to 375° F and simmer for 20 minutes. Remove from grill and allow to cool slightly.

6. Reduce heat on grill to 225° F. Season the tomahawk steak with Chop House Steak Rub on both sides. Place the steak on the grill grates, insert a temperature probe, and grill, undisturbed, for 45 minutes, or until the steak reaches an internal temperature of 120°F

7. Remove steak from grill and set aside. Open the Sear Slide on your and increase temperature to 400°F. Return tomahawk to grill and sear over open flames, about 2-3 minutes per side.

8. Pull the steak off the grill and allow it to rest for 10 minutes. Ladle reserved apple butter over steak and serve.

Marinated Flank Steak

Servings: 6

Cooking Time: 10 Minutes

Ingredients:

- 2lb (1kg) flank steak
- coarse salt
- freshly ground black pepper
- for the marinade
- ¼ cup red wine vinegar
- 2 tbsp Worcestershire sauce
- 1½ tsp coarse salt
- ½ cup extra virgin olive oil
- 2 garlic cloves, peeled and smashed with a chef's knife
- 1 small white onion, coarsely chopped
- 2 tbsp finely chopped fresh rosemary leaves
- sprigs of fresh rosemary

Directions:

1. In a jar with a tight-fitting lid, make the marinade by combining the vinegar, Worcestershire sauce, salt, and olive oil. Shake vigorously. Stir in the garlic, onion, and rosemary leaves.

2. Place the flank steak in a resealable plastic bag and pour the marinade over it. Turn the steak to thoroughly coat. Refrigerate for 8 to 24 hours, turning the bag periodically to thoroughly marinate the steak.

3. Supply your smoker with wood pellets and follow the start-up procedure. Preheat the grill, with the lid closed, to 232° F.

4. Remove the steak from the marinade and pat dry with paper towels. (Discard the marinade.) Season on both sides with salt and pepper.

5. Place the steak on the grate and grill until the internal temperature reaches 125 to 135°F (52 to 54°C), about 4 to 5 minutes per side.

6. Remove the steak from the grill and let rest for 5 minutes. Slice thinly against the grain with a knife held on a sharp diagonal. Transfer the slices to a platter and scatter rosemary sprigs over the top before serving.